This is Citizenship

second edition

Teacher's Resource Book

1

Julia Fiehn
Terry Fiehn

DL DYNAMIC LEARNING
Innovate · Motivate · Personalise

HODDER EDUCATION
PART OF HACHETTE LIVRE UK

The Publishers would like to thank the following for permission to reproduce copyright material:
Photo credits: **p.58** *All* © Fairtrade Foundation

Although every effort has been made to ensure that website addresses are correct at time of going to press, Hodder Education cannot be held responsible for the content of any website mentioned in this book. It is sometimes possible to find a relocated web page by typing in the address of the home page for a website in the URL window of your browser.

Hachette Livre UK's policy is to use papers that are natural, renewable and recyclable products and made from wood grown in sustainable forests. The logging and manufacturing processes are expected to conform to the environmental regulations of the country of origin.

Orders: please contact Bookpoint Ltd, 130 Milton Park, Abingdon, Oxon OX14 4SB. Telephone: (44) 01235 827720. Fax: (44) 01235 400454. Lines are open 9.00 a.m.–5.00 p.m., Monday to Saturday, with a 24-hour message answering service. Visit our website at www.hoddereducation.co.uk

© Terry Fiehn, Julia Fiehn 2008
First published in 2008 by
Hodder Education,
Part of Hachette Livre UK
338 Euston Road
London NW1 3BH

Impression number   5 4 3 2 1
Year   2012 2011 2010 2009 2008

All rights reserved. Apart from any use permitted under UK copyright law, the material in this publication is copyright and cannot be photocopied or otherwise produced in its entirety or copied onto acetate without permission. Electronic copying is not permitted. Permission is given to teachers to make limited copies of the activity sheets, for classroom distribution only, to students within their own school or educational institution. The material may not be copied in full, in unlimited quantities, kept on behalf of others, distributed outside the purchasing institution, copied onwards, sold to third parties, or stored for future use in a retrieval system. This permission is subject to the payment of the purchase price of the book. If you wish to use the material in any way other than as specified you must apply in writing to the Publisher at the above address.

Illustrations by Barking Dog Art and Karen Donnelly
Typeset in Frutiger Roman 11/14pt by Fakenham Photosetting, Norfolk
Printed in Great Britain by Hobbs The Printers, Totton, Hants

A catalogue record for this title is available from the British Library

ISBN: 978 0340 947104

Other titles in the series

This is Citizenship 1 Pupil's Book: 978 0340 947098
This is Citizenship 1 Teacher's Resource: 978 0340 947104
This is Citizenship 1 Dynamic Learning: 978 0340 947111

This is Citizenship 2 Pupil's Book: 978 0340 947128
This is Citizenship 2 Teacher's Resource: 978 0340 947135
This is Citizenship 2 Dynamic Learning: 978 0340 947142

This is Citizenship 3 Pupil's Book: 978 0340 947159
This is Citizenship 3 Teacher's Resource: 978 0340 947166
This is Citizenship 3 Dynamic Learning: 978 0340 947173

Contents

INTRODUCTION		v
About the series		v
Using Pupil's Book 1		xii

Detailed notes and Activity sheets

SECTION 1:	Rules and fairness, rights and responsibilities	2
SECTION 2:	Communities and identities	23
SECTION 3:	Being a global citizen	41
Resources		72

Introduction

About the series

This series is designed to cover the knowledge, skills and understanding laid down in the citizenship orders and incorporated in the revised programme of study for Key Stage 3 from autumn 2008. There are four books in the series which, taken together, form part of a coherent approach to citizenship across years 7 to 11 and beyond.

Key Stage 3

- *This is Citizenship 1* is a foundation book aimed at years 7 and 8.
- *This is Citizenship 2*, aimed at years 8 and 9, builds on the skills and understanding developed in Book 1 and introduces more topics in the Key Stage 3 programme of study.
- *This is Citizenship 3,* aimed at year 9, provides further coverage of the new Key Stage 3 Citizenship requirements.

Key Stage 4 and post-16

- *Citizenship Studies for GCSE and Key Stage 4* is aimed at years 10 and 11 and is designed for pupils taking GCSE examinations in citizenship as well as for those who are taking unexamined courses in Key Stage 4. It can also be used on post-16 citizenship courses.

The books are designed as flexible resources to meet your needs and those of your pupils. They aim to provide high-quality activities and learning materials that will form a platform on which you can construct your own citizenship programmes. The books contain ideas for approaches to the statutory knowledge, skills and understanding of citizenship that will engage and motivate pupils. These approaches draw on the techniques of active learning, group work and pupil investigations in order to involve pupils in their own learning – an essential feature of citizenship programmes. Teachers are encouraged to work with local organisations and other people and to bring the subject to life by using local issues and real-world case studies.

Progression

Each book consists of sections or self-contained units that can be used in any order. Although there is no deliberate plan of progression between the units, pupils do develop their skills and understanding as they work their way through the book. They should be able to build their skills as they progress but this can also be done if the units, or elements of them, are used in a different order or different way.

There is progression between books, and it is hoped that pupils will develop and refine their concept of citizenship as they move through the series. Books 1, 2 and 3 cover citizenship at Key Stage 3. Book 1 provides the groundwork. The level of information is more detailed in Books 2 and 3. This should help pupils to gain greater knowledge and understanding of institutions, for example parliament, local government and the judiciary, and of citizenship issues such as rights and laws. More complex issues and concepts are introduced in Books 2 and 3, for example conflicting rights, political parties and pressure groups. Usually this means that pupils will need higher order skills to handle these issues and concepts.

Citizenship Studies for GCSE and Key Stage 4 continues this process but in the context of the specifications laid down by the awarding bodies for Key Stage 4 and of non-examination courses. It also revisits some of the areas in the earlier books to reinforce understanding and explore topics in more complex contexts.

This is Citizenship 1 Teacher's Resource Book

Introduction

Content matched with programme of study for Key Stage 3 Citizenship		
Content	Key concepts	Key processes
Section 1: Rules and fairness, rights and responsibilities **Rules** **Fairness** **Children's rights and responsibilities** **Having a say and school councils** **Developing debating skills**	1.1 Democracy and justice a. Participating actively in different kinds of decision-making and voting in order to influence public life b. Weighing up what is fair and unfair in different situations 1.2 Rights and responsibilities a. Exploring different kinds of rights and obligations and how these affect both individuals and communities c. Investigating ways in which rights can compete and conflict, and understanding that hard decisions have to be made to try to balance these	2.1 Critical thinking and enquiry Pupils should be able to: a. engage with and reflect on different ideas, opinions, beliefs and values when exploring topical and controversial issues and problems 2.2 Advocacy and representation Pupils should be able to: a. express and explain their own opinions to others through discussions, formal debates and voting c. justify their argument, giving reasons to try to persuade others to think again, change or support them d. represent the views of others, with which they may or may not agree 2.3 Taking informed and responsible action Pupils should be able to: a. explore creative approaches to taking action on problems and issues to achieve intended purposes

This is Citizenship 1 Teacher's Resource Book

Introduction

Content matched with programme of study for Key Stage 3 Citizenship		
Content	Key concepts	Key processes
Section 2: Communities and identities **Belonging to a community** **Different identities** **Living together in communities** **Improving your town centre** **Changing things** **Bringing communities together** **Making communities sustainable** **Developing research skills**	1.1 Democracy and justice c. Considering how democracy, justice, diversity, toleration, respect and freedom are valued by people with different beliefs, backgrounds and traditions within a changing democratic society 1.2 Rights and responsibilities c. Investigating ways in which rights can compete and conflict, and understanding that hard decisions have to be made to try to balance these 1.3 Identities and diversity: living together in the UK a. Appreciating that identities are complex, can change over time and are informed by different understandings of what it means to be a citizen in the UK b. Exploring the diverse national, regional, ethnic and religious cultures, groups and communities in the UK and the connections between them d. Exploring community cohesion	2.1 Critical thinking and enquiry Pupils should be able to: a. engage with and reflect on different ideas, opinions, beliefs and values when exploring topical and controversial issues and problems b. research, plan and undertake enquiries into issues and problems 2.2 Advocacy and representation Pupils should be able to: a. express and explain their own opinions to others through discussions b. communicate an argument, taking account of different viewpoints and drawing on what they have learnt through research, action and debate 2.3 Taking informed and responsible action Pupils should be able to: a. explore creative approaches to taking action on problems and issues to achieve intended purposes b. analyse the impact of their actions on communities c. reflect on the progress they have made

This is Citizenship 1 Teacher's Resource Book

Introduction

Content matched with programme of study for Key Stage 3 Citizenship		
Content	Key concepts	Key processes
Section 3: Being a global citizen **Our connections with other countries** **Images of rich and poor countries in the world** **Child labour** **Fair trade** **The work of charities** **The impact of tourism** **Developing campaigning skills**	1.1 Democracy and justice b. Weighing up what is fair and unfair in different situations 1.2 Rights and responsibilities a. Exploring different kinds of rights and obligations and how these affect both individuals and communities c. Investigating ways in which rights can compete and conflict, and understanding that hard decisions have to be made to try to balance these	2.1 Critical thinking and enquiry Pupils should be able to: a. engage with and reflect on different ideas, opinions, beliefs and values when exploring topical and controversial issues and problems b. research, plan and undertake enquiries into issues and problems 2.2 Advocacy and representation Pupils should be able to: a. express and explain their own opinions to others through discussions, formal debates and voting b. communicate an argument, taking account of different viewpoints and drawing on what they have learnt through research, action and debate d. represent the views of others, with which they may or may not agree 2.3 Taking informed and responsible action Pupils should be able to: a. explore creative approaches to taking action on problems and issues to achieve intended purposes b. work individually and with others to negotiate, plan and take action on citizenship issues and try to influence others

Introduction

Education for citizenship

Bernard Crick has written: 'Citizenship is more than a statutory subject. If taught well and tailored to local needs, its skills and values will enhance democratic life for us all, both rights and responsibilities, beginning in school and radiating out' (*Citizenship and the Teaching of Democracy in Schools*, 1998).

The Secretary of State for Education has said, 'Education in citizenship and democracy will provide coherence in the way in which all pupils are helped to develop a full understanding of their roles and responsibilities as citizens in a modern democracy. It will play an important role, alongside other aspects of the curriculum and school life, in helping pupils to deal with difficult moral and social questions that arise in their lives and in society' (Introduction to the *National Curriculum Handbook for Citizenship*, DfEE/QCA 1999).

Three interrelated strands for teaching citizenship have been identified:

- social and moral responsibility, which involves pupils learning about their behaviour towards others and developing self-confidence
- community involvement, through which pupils can participate positively with others in their neighbourhood and learn how to become helpfully involved in their local communities
- political literacy, which involves pupils developing their understanding of the workings of democratic systems (institutions, issues and problems) and the skills and values required to participate themselves.

Following a review of the Curriculum by Sir Keith Ajegbo, a fourth strand has been introduced. This involves an understanding of issues of identity (or a sense of belonging) and diversity, approached 'through a political and historical lens'. (*Diversity and Citizenship*, Dfes 2007).

Citizenship is a complex concept embracing a number of different elements. At one level, citizenship is a legal status that gives an individual certain rights and obligations in the state of which he or she is recognised as a citizen. This legal status is determined in different ways in different countries. It might depend on place of birth, parentage, application or even passing a test as in the United States. The rights and duties associated with citizenship also vary from one country to another; for instance, in some countries voting is regarded as a duty and it is against the law not to vote. People's rights and duties might depend on their sex, and all countries have different laws for adults and children.

However, citizenship is widely regarded as more than a legal status. It also involves behaviour towards others, taking responsibility for one's actions and caring for the well-being of other people; it encompasses the role we play in the local community and the way we obey laws. The interesting questions about citizenship arise when there are legitimate disagreements about these areas, for example:

- Is it legitimate to break the law during a protest?
- What constitutes reasonable and acceptable behaviour or anti-social behaviour?
- How far is the individual or the state responsible for elderly people in the community?
- How far should freedom of the press go?

The distinction between areas such as freedom and authority, rights and responsibility, democracy and dictatorship is often blurred. Pupils can only develop their understanding of these difficult concepts if they are exposed to real issues that examine the boundaries of their application in a range of contexts.

Citizenship is also a very broad concept. At one end, it is about the immediate environment in which people live. It is to do with people contributing to their communities, improving the environment and helping others – or not doing any of these things. At the other end, the idea of global citizenship is becoming increasingly important as we grow more aware that our actions can affect people in other countries,

This is Citizenship 1 Teacher's Resource Book

Introduction

for example in terms of the environment, sustainability and global warming or the way goods are traded with other countries.

The aim of the books in this series is to help pupils to develop their own notion of citizenship and what it entails over the course of their secondary education. There is no attempt to predetermine or constrain what is taught in citizenship courses; it is for teachers to determine their citizenship programmes according to their own principles and school ethos as well as the needs of their pupils and the community in which they live. Our aim is to produce stimulating materials that will engage pupils in discussion about some of the key issues involved in citizenship and encourage them to be active participants. Citizenship education is much more than learning about how political systems, local government, etc. operate. It is about giving pupils the knowledge and skills to be able to play a role in democratic processes at different levels from the neighbourhood up to national level. In a citizenship course it is therefore vital that pupils play an active part in their own learning so that they can transfer their skills and the confidence this brings to whatever public arena they enter.

Delivery

Citizenship can form part of many aspects of the school curriculum, and each school will have its own approach to delivery. It is an integral part of personal, social and health education and there are many overlapping issues in religious education, careers education and guidance, and tutorial work. Some aspects of citizenship can be covered in geography, history and English. In addition, a number of elements of the wider curriculum will also help to deliver citizenship knowledge, skills and understanding. These might include a school council, community projects, charity work, enterprise activities, various off-timetable events, residential experiences and awards such as the Duke of Edinburgh's Award Scheme. In particular, citizenship should reflect, and be reflected in, the values and ethos of the school.

Citizenship can be delivered in three main ways, although these are not mutually exclusive:

- as a discrete area of the curriculum
- through other subjects
- through special events and activities.

Evidence from QCA monitoring, Ofsted inspections and other observation suggests that to be delivered effectively citizenship needs some discrete time, preferably taught by a team of teachers who are interested in the subject and committed to the aims and objectives of citizenship education. This is especially the case with aspects of citizenship such as the law and justice, political systems or the working of local government which are not easy to fit in with other subject areas. The main aspect missing in the citizenship programme of many schools is political literacy and this is one of the main strands identified by Bernard Crick. Without this aspect, citizenship is a hollow subject.

However, other aspects will overlap with a comprehensive PSHE course or tutorial programme, for example rights and responsibilities and conflict resolution. Some topics are recognised subject matter of other curriculum areas, for example the role of the media in English or development studies in geography. Special school events and activities, for example an environment day or multi-cultural festival, develop the skills of involvement and participation that underpin active citizenship. These events are probably already part of the normal school year but have not always been recognised as vehicles for the delivery of the knowledge, skills and attitudes required for citizenship.

Most citizenship courses will use all three methods of delivery. Many schools will decide to teach citizenship as one component of a PSHE programme with links to other parts of the PSHE programme and to other subject areas. The citizenship programme will need to be co-ordinated by a post-holder who has an overview of the ways in which citizenship is provided across the whole curriculum. This person might be

This is Citizenship 1 Teacher's Resource Book

Introduction

a member of staff who has, or is willing to develop, particular interest and expertise in the area. It is essential to have someone in place who can provide information, training and guidance for other staff and who leads on matters of curriculum development.

The books in this series have been designed to work with all of these methods of delivery. The various sections of the books can be taught as discrete units. Alternatively, activities can be lifted out to slip into the PSHE programme or into other subjects. They have been constructed for maximum flexibility to cater for the many different ways in which citizenship is taught.

Controversial issues, balance and bias

Many of the topics covered in the citizenship curriculum are likely to be of a controversial and sensitive nature. Detailed guidance on teaching controversial issues is provided by QCA in *Citizenship at Key Stages 3 and 4 – initial guidance for schools*, QCA, 2000, and in the QCA teacher's guide for citizenship at KS3. It is important not to try to shelter pupils from controversial issues that are an integral part of social life. Pupils should be encouraged to develop the appropriate skills to understand and deal with them: listening, arguing a case, accepting others' points of view, dealing with conflict and distinguishing fact from opinion.

It is also important, however, that teachers do not expose any individual children to expressions of intolerance, prejudice or hostility. A classroom ethos should be encouraged that allows pupils to express opinions in a manner respectful of others' feelings. Teachers should also aim to provide a balance of views in order to prevent bias in teaching. Again, pupils need to be given the chance to learn the skills that will help them to recognise bias. In addition, however, teachers should not emphasise selected information, present information as incontrovertible, set themselves up as authorities, reveal their own preferences and views unless it is appropriate or use materials from some organisations with a particular viewpoint while ignoring others with a different viewpoint. None of this implies that racist or other discriminatory views should be acceptable. Teachers should make clear that certain forms of behaviour are not tolerated.

The Revised Programme of Study for Key Stage 3

The secondary curriculum has been reviewed in order to increase flexibility in the curriculum and enable schools to better meet the needs of young people. The new curriculum has been designed to develop:

- 'successful learners who enjoy learning, make progress and achieve;
- confident individuals who are able to live safe, healthy and fulfilling lives; and
- responsible citizens who make a positive contribution to society'.

There is a three-year implementation period for the new curriculum from 2008 to 2011. All National Curriculum subjects share a common format for their revised programmes of study, consisting of an 'importance statement', key concepts, key processes and curriculum opportunities.

For citizenship, the importance statement reflects the original three strands (social and moral responsibility, community involvement and political literacy) and also lays renewed emphasis on the last of these by stressing the importance of action: '[Young people] learn to take part in decision-making and different forms of action. They play an active role in the life of their schools, neighbourhoods, communities and wider society as active and global citizens.'

Revision of the programmes of study for citizenship has provided an opportunity to restate the nature of the subject and clarify its relationship with other, related areas of study, such as personal, social and health education. The key concepts and processes underline its distinctiveness. The key citizenship concepts are:

This is Citizenship 1 Teacher's Resource Book

Introduction

- democracy and justice
- rights and responsibilities
- identities and diversity.

The key processes are:

- critical thinking and enquiry
- advocacy and representation
- taking informed and responsible action.

The curriculum opportunities for citizenship include a wide range of active learning likely to enthuse and engage young people, such as debates, role play and community-based activities, and that draw on the expertise and concerns of members of the local community.

Using Pupil's Book 1

This is not a textbook in the traditional sense. We do not expect classes to work steadily through the entire book, although some of the units can be worked through in this way. Rather it is a series of activities designed to cover the skills, knowledge and understanding laid down in the citizenship programme of study. It can be used in a variety of contexts and offers a pragmatic approach to course planning. It provides:

- a range of activities that can be taught in short time slots of around 30–40 minutes or longer exercises that can be broken down into shorter component parts
- a base of activities on which you can build your own self-determined citizenship programme
- active learning to engage pupils and promote pupil participation
- activities that require relatively little physical preparation.

The activities in the Pupil's Book can be used as they stand; the information provided is sufficient for the activities to work. However, some teachers may wish to extend the active nature of the tasks by providing cards for sorting or role cards for the simulations. To support this, resource sheets for photocopying and cutting up are provided in this Teacher's Resource Book. Also, some additional activities are suggested together with activity sheets to support them.

Within units some activities do build on others. Some of these activities are progressive in difficulty or complexity, while others are not. Most activities can be inserted into courses when and where you think they are appropriate and meet your needs and those of your pupils.

The topics and activities in Book 1 are aimed broadly at pupils in years 7 and 8. However, teachers will use the materials in different ways and at different times – lessons have to fit in with whole-school programmes of work and the needs of the pupils. Some of the activities could also be used with pupils in year 9 – it depends very much on the class, the abilities of the pupils and the work being done in other areas of the curriculum.

Hard-pressed teachers will find it difficult to gather all the resources and materials needed to teach citizenship courses. This book is designed to save you time and energy by providing a core of activities and resources to which your own ideas and local variants can be added. In this way you will be able to build up your own individualised programme. The authors hope that pupils will find the activities stimulating, engaging and enjoyable.

Detailed notes

Section 1: Rules and fairness, rights and responsibilities

Section 1: Rules and fairness, rights and responsibilities

Aim of section

This section is designed to introduce pupils to some of the basic requirements for living in groups and, therefore, of citizenship: rules, sanctions, punishments and fairness. Pupils of this age are often very concerned about fairness, and the section looks at the difficulties of ensuring fairness when rules are applied. Once pupils have examined rules, punishments and the difficulties of applying rules fairly, they are ready to look at laws and lawmaking. Pupils using this book in year 7 will be new to their secondary school, and teachers often use PSHE lessons to introduce them to the expectations of the school. This section can be used within PSHE as part of pupils' induction to their new school, and to raise wider issues of citizenship.

The second part of the section focuses on rights and responsibilities – key concepts in citizenship. Here, these are considered in a more personal way related to the world of the children. The topic of human rights in a wider context is examined in more depth in Books 2 and 3. There is a particular emphasis on the responsibilities that young people have in relation to those around them and to others in the wider community in preparation for them taking responsible action – a theme pursued further on in the book. In this section, we relate responsible action to pupil participation in the running of schools and learner voice. School councils are introduced in order to provide a forum for pupils to take part in debates and to learn about the operation of democracy. The aim at the end of the section is to focus directly on those all important skills concerned with expressing and justifying opinions and developing an argument.

CITIZENSHIP PROGRAMME OF STUDY

This section covers the following concepts and processes:

Key concepts

1.1 Democracy and justice
a. Participating actively in different kinds of decision-making and voting in order to influence public life
b. Weighing up what is fair and unfair in different situations

1.2 Rights and responsibilities
a. Exploring different kinds of rights and obligations and how these affect both individuals and communities
c. Investigating ways in which rights can compete and conflict, and understanding that hard decisions have to be made to try to balance these

Key processes

2.1 Critical thinking and enquiry
   Pupils should be able to:
a. engage with and reflect on different ideas, opinions, beliefs and values when exploring topical and controversial issues and problems

2.2 Advocacy and representation
Pupils should be able to:
a. express and explain their own opinions to others through discussions, formal debates and voting
c. justify their argument, giving reasons to try to persuade others to think again, change or support them
d. represent the views of others, with which they may or may not agree

2.3 Taking informed and responsible action
   Pupils should be able to:
a. explore creative approaches to taking action on problems and issues to achieve intended purposes

Section 1: Rules and fairness, rights and responsibilities

1.1 Would you like to go to school on Hoff?

Pupil's Book pp. 2–3

Planet Hoff is used as a fun way to introduce a discussion of rules and punishments. It presents an extreme example of a system of school punishments in which the tariffs are known to all and are applied in all cases of rule infringement. However, the only evidence required is the word of a member of authority and there is no appeal against the punishment. Pupils are asked to discuss the fairness of such a system and compare it to their own. They learn about the concept of fairness by applying it in real and imagined situations. Some schools in the UK are using more tightly defined discipline structures and a few use a points system for punishment, although they would not be as inflexible as the system in Zap High School. However, the **Activity** gives pupils a chance to discuss the merits of different discipline systems and this is usually a topic on which they have a lot to say.

1.2 Are school rules fair?

Pupil's Book pp. 4–7
Activity sheets 1, 2

This spread examines the need for rules in any social group, but particularly in a school. You can make use of the illustrations on pages 4–5, which highlight some of the issues – unruly behaviour in corridors, bullying, pupils behaving badly in the classroom with the teacher present. You should provide your class with a copy of your school rules or home–school contract for question 1 on page 4. If these are not written down, you could ask pupils in a quick brainstorm to list the main school rules. This would be an interesting exercise in itself to find out what they understand the rules to be, how they interpret them and what they think about them. If you don't wish to focus on your own school, you could use the set of rules on **Activity sheet 1**.

Page 5 Make your own class ground rules for discussions

Many tutor groups or classes in primary and secondary schools are encouraged to develop their own rules or 'contract' of behaviour, usually as part of PSHE lessons. The aim is to help pupils to see rules as necessary for harmonious relations and in everyone's interests, rather than just imposed by an external authority. It is essential in any classroom where citizenship discussions take place that there is an agreed set of ground rules so that all pupils get a chance to participate and discussions are not dominated by a small group of pupils.

To make sure all pupils are involved in drawing up the rules, the **Activity** uses the technique of 'consensus-building', in which pupils work first in pairs, then in small groups and finally as a whole class, to come to agreement about the rules they will follow in class. The statement starters can be used as a framework for the pupils. However, they may wish to add their own statements, or cut some from the list.

Pages 6–7 If you were the teacher ...

This spread pursues the theme of rules and punishments but from a different perspective. Pupils are asked to consider their application from the teacher's point of view. This is a decision-making exercise which encourages pupils to realise that making quick decisions is not easy and that the outcomes may not always be entirely fair. It is important that the pupils are encouraged to give reasons for their decisions. This is partly because the application of rules in school (and sometimes in society at large) is sometimes seen as arbitrary by young people and they need to understand that there is a rational process behind a system of rules, albeit that this is not always apparent. But it is also because pupils, as part of their development of citizenship skills, should start to give reasons for their opinions.

This is Citizenship 1 Teacher's Resource Book

Section 1: Rules and fairness, rights and responsibilities

Activity sheet 2 supports this spread. It sets out Jenny Bennett's decisions so that pupils can write in their responses to each decision with a reason. These can then be used to prompt discussion. Question 3 raises the issue of fairness, which is the focus of the following spreads. In some of their responses, the pupils will almost certainly have mentioned fairness. So you can now say that you are going to look at the concept of fairness directly.

1.3 It's not fair!

Pupil's Book pp. 8–13
Activity sheets 3, 4

This section looks explicitly at the notion of fairness and aims to show that fairness for everyone can be difficult to achieve in everyday life, whether in a school, a family or society at large. Pupils often complain that they have been treated unfairly, because they believe that they have not been at fault. The **Activity** on page 8 shows how, whether or not Sam was at fault, he/she suffered from various punishments, and these had further consequences for Sam. Sam can be male or female. The character is deliberately not shown, although some pupils will assume Sam is female.

Pupils should use the bullet list on page 8 to decide how fair each punishment was and try to come to some conclusions about what is fair and what is not. This is also an opportunity to ask pupils to consider that actions have consequences even if the actions were not intended. The main outcome of the discussion is likely to be that, when rules are imposed, it is not always possible to give everyone a fair deal.

Pages 10–11 Who will go to the TV studio?

In the **Activity**, pupils themselves have to make decisions that others may regard as unfair. They experience a situation in which many teachers have found themselves: they have to choose six pupils to receive a prize that has been won by the whole class. Each case illustrates a different reason why someone should be given preferential treatment, and the pupils have to consider each reason before coming to their own decisions. They should be encouraged to make these decisions, even though they might decide early on that drawing lots or voting for the winners would be fairer. Sometimes even drawing lots or voting results in some people being treated unfairly, because of some individuals' popularity or past circumstances not being taken into account. It is, in fact, very difficult to decide which six should go and this should create some intense debate when brought to a class discussion to reach final agreement. This should help pupils to realise that an 'absolutely fair' decision cannot be arrived at and that this reflects what happens in real life.

Activity sheet 3 can be used to help pupils to prioritise the different cases. Photocopy the statements from the Activity sheet and cut them up so that each pair of pupils has one set of cards. Pupils can then physically manipulate the cards during their discussions.

1 Ask pupils to arrange the cards in order of importance.
2 Ask them to sort the cards into two piles: good reasons for being chosen and reasons that are not so good.
3 Ask each pupil to choose one of the statements and then argue that case with his or her partner.

Pages 12–13 What's the fairest way to give pupils places in secondary schools?

This spread explores the concept of fairness in the context of a major citizenship issue. It is designed to show pupils that fairness is a central concept in many of the big decisions made in society. The allocation of school places and how fair the system operates is, of course, an issue which takes centre stage at particular times, but it is a controversial one at local and national level that is hotly debated more or less continuously. It is also an issue which is relevant to the pupils themselves and one which they know about. It has a profound effect on the

This is Citizenship 1 Teacher's Resource Book

Section 1: Rules and fairness, rights and responsibilities

young citizens in the UK and can determine their future life chances. This can be a controversial issue in the classroom and should be handled sensitively.

The idea of the lottery was put forward in Brighton, although at the time of writing not acted upon, but more recently a number of commentators have suggested that it should be given serious consideration nationally. The notion behind it is that a lottery is inherently a fairer method of allocating places because there is no scope for parents, and indeed schools, to manipulate the system and control the sort of pupils going to so-called 'good' schools.

Here it is used as a concrete example to encourage the pupils to consider the different methods used to place pupils in secondary schools and to think about the fairest way of managing the process. It poses the classic dilemma of fairness: a resource, in this case school places, is limited and you have to establish how to decide who gets this resource. **Activity sheet 4** can be used to help pupils work out the pros and cons of different ways of sorting out places. Make clear to them that they can arrive at a solution which uses a combination of methods, for example siblings first, then lottery.

We have deliberately not put independent schools into the mix as this can take the argument off into a completely different direction and we want to focus clearly on the allocation of school places in the state sector. There is of course no reason why the teacher should not develop this as a separate discussion.

1.4 What rights should all children have?

Pupil's Book pp. 14–15
Activity sheets 5, 6

This spread looks at children's rights. As a prelude to this you might like to use **Activity sheet 5** which sets the scene for the main **Activity** on pages 14–15. It asks pupils to draw up their own charter of rights. It is likely that young people will draw up charters that give them unfettered rights. Discussion of the charters should include recognition of the individual responsibilities that young people have to their peers and to relevant adults if the charters are to be followed.

The main **Activity** on page 14 asks pupils to list the rights that they think all children should have. **Activity sheet 6** provides a template for this Activity. The discussion should take pupils beyond simplistic answers and help them to consider children from all walks of life and from all countries of the world. Discussion should also help them to see that some of the rights might conflict. For example, the right to work can prevent children from engaging in full-time education. The bubbles provide some suggestions, but you could encourage pupils to add more rights if they can think of them. They should also think about child protection issues and those aspects of life that children should be protected from (for example, alcohol, abuse, getting into debt).

1.5 No man is an island . . .

Pupil's Book pp. 16–17

This spread introduces the notion of responsibilities. In the first part of the **Activity**, pupils are asked to rank people according to how much responsibility they consider they have towards them. This has been put in terms of the people they would help most if they were in difficulty. One would expect pupils to rank them by giving priority to people closest to them but this may not always be the case. Then they are put in situations where there is a conflict of responsibilities and where they might decide to adopt a position which conflicts with their responses in the first question.

This aims to make them aware of the responsibilities we have towards other people (and more particularly to the wider community) and that it is not easy to decide

This is Citizenship 1 Teacher's Resource Book

Section 1: Rules and fairness, rights and responsibilities

how to act because difficult choices are involved. Often this means giving up something we might want or going against people we are close to. Some pupils might decide their closest ties to family and friends are more important no matter what the choice presented to them. They may not feel they can break the conventions of their groups. There are no right answers here but rather difficult choices, often the case in real life. Two key issues to pick up in discussion are:

- What responsibility, if any, do we have towards other people?
- Is our responsibility towards friends and family different from our responsibility towards people we don't know?

The famous poem at the end of the spread, by John Donne and written in 1624, captures the idea that human beings are bound together, that the human race is larger than its constituent parts. In the full version of the poem, it suggests that every death affects every one of us, and so when someone dies, the funeral bell 'tolls for me'. Pupils may not have heard of Hemingway's novel, *For Whom the Bell Tolls*, whose title comes from the poem, but you could discuss the themes of war, brutality and brotherhood that are expressed within it. Or you could engage the pupils in a discussion of the many divisions in our world (national, political, religious, ethnic), and whether people could relate better than they do to those of different origins.

1.6 Whose responsibility?

Pupil's Book pp. 18–21
Activity sheets 7, 8, 9, 10A, 10B, 11

The **Activity** on page 19 is designed to deepen pupils' understanding of the notion of responsibilities and to encourage them to think about the general responsibilities people have to each other in the local community in an everyday context. A visual approach has been adopted to make the Activity more engaging and more accessible to all pupils. The illustrations in the scenes are very detailed and should be examined carefully by pupils in order to spot what is happening.

Each scene focuses on a different aspect of life in a community and raises questions about responsible and irresponsible behaviour. For example, in the park, the park keeper has the responsibility to make sure that the park is safe and clean for everyone. The dog owner should use a 'pooper-scooper' to protect young children from disease. The parents should keep an eye on their children. In the shopping centre, security staff have a responsibility to stop thieves, to help if someone is lost and to prevent vandalism. Shopkeepers should serve customers politely and should sell goods in a manner that is within the law. In the street scene, the cyclist has a responsibility to make sure he does not hurt other people if riding on the pavement, the girls crossing the road are responsible for their own safety, as are the car driver and the motorcyclist, who might not be aware of them, and so on. There are many discussion points in this illustration. The drawings should also help pupils to consider the consequences of actions.

The quiz on pages 20–21 (reproduced on **Activity sheet 7** to hand out) is designed to take the notion of responsibility a stage further by making pupils aware that they can take positive action themselves to do something about situations in which they find themselves. This is the first stage towards active citizenship. However, not all these situations are straightforward and there can be pressures (peer pressure, personal safety) that prevent people from acting, particularly when they are younger. There are a number of issues to pick up:

- What rights do we have to become involved in other people's actions?
- What duties do we have?
- Do we worry that other people will think us boring if we are responsible?
- Do we worry that we will fall out with our friends? That they will call us names?

As a follow-up, ask pupils to decide on three occasions when someone would have no

This is Citizenship 1 Teacher's Resource Book

Section 1: Rules and fairness, rights and responsibilities

option but to intervene in a situation, whether they wanted to or not. For example, in France it is against the law *not* to help someone who has had an accident. Should this be the case in this country? Should you report a crime that you witness? Should people keep an eye on their own neighbourhood, as in Neighbourhood Watch schemes?

Learning to be assertive

Young people can find it very difficult to take responsible action. They do not know how to go about it and they are worried about the response they get from their peers and other people. So they may find it helpful to do a little work on learning how to behave in these circumstances. Assertiveness is a form of behaviour in which people recognise their own and other people's rights in any situation. It means respecting other people and reaching solutions to difficult problems by being calm, clear and honest.

Activity sheet 8 can be used to help pupils to practise assertive behaviour. The sheet also suggests an extension activity in which pupils have to think about times when they have not behaved assertively.

Activity sheets 9, 10A, 10B and **11** consider other aspects of assertiveness and could also be used as part of a wider programme seeking to encourage pupils to be more assertive in their behaviour and thereby more confident in their interactions inside and outside school.

1.7 Having a say

Pupil's Book pp. 22–25

If citizenship education is going to be effective, then it needs to be part of the culture of the school. This means that pupils should have a greater say in the running of the school and should be consulted on all sorts of issues including teaching and learning. There is now a growing body of research to suggest that learner voice can play a positive part in school improvement and in creating a positive pupil orientation towards the school as an organisation. This spread asks pupils to consider the areas in which they might 'have a say' and where the boundaries might be. We have deliberately not put in consultation on curriculum or teaching and learning in this exercise – this might be something for later. However, a lot of schools are establishing advisory councils on curriculum and consulting pupils on what worked well and what did not in particular units of work.

The **Activity** also asks pupils to think about the skills involved in learner voice because pupils gain a great deal in terms of citizenship skills by being involved in consultative processes. The end of the spread raises the question of ways that pupils can be involved in the running of the school. The school council is the most obvious and most common, but some institutions, particularly those for older pupils, are using technology-based methods, for example electronic voting and texting, to involve more pupils in decision-making. Some schools are using online voting to elect representatives and consult pupils on a range of school issues. You can have a look at one web program, mi-voice-democracy, enabled at www.mi-voice.com.

On a less adventurous scale, you might consider running a classroom council as a forum for holding meetings and airing problems and grievances. It can be a useful way of helping pupils to experience and familiarise themselves with some basic democratic procedures. It is also a simple way of introducing the idea of a constitution as well as the formal rules of debate and of practising how to run a meeting.

Pages 24–25 Who represents your views at school?

This spread is designed to raise pupils' awareness of their school council and what it does in the school. It may be helpful to bring in an older pupil who is a member of the school council to answer questions about its operation. The question also encourages pupils to look at some of the complaints about the way the school

This is Citizenship 1 Teacher's Resource Book

Section 1: Rules and fairness, rights and responsibilities

council operates. It is important to address these if pupils feel disenchanted with the process in operation. It may be that the school needs to ensure that its school council works democratically, particularly since an important aspect of the citizenship curriculum is to teach about democratic procedures. Certainly, it should look at how pupils can make a genuine contribution and explain to them why it is unlikely that real power will be handed over to them. Question 3 on page 25 looks at ways in which the school council can be improved. Advice and guidance about the operation of school councils is available from School Councils website, whose address is listed in the Resources section of this Teacher's Resource Book.

1.8 Taking part in a debate

Pupil's Book pp. 26–29

An important aim of citizenship education is to develop pupils' skills of expressing opinions, making reasoned arguments and being able to respond to the arguments of others in debate. This is clearly a long-term process and we hope that by the end of their school life pupils will be articulate and able to state their position on a range of issues and therefore be able to play an active role in public life. Many of the activities in this book are designed to provide pupils with opportunities to express their views and support these with reasons. These two spreads introduce some of the structures of the formal debate through which pupils can develop their arguing skills. In Books 2 and 3, there will be subsections which focus on taking their arguing and debating skills to higher levels, for example evaluating arguments, making a reasoned case for a particular position and so on. Of course, pupils will not be starting from scratch: many primary schools are extremely good at encouraging their pupils in debating and public speaking. So you can use this as an opportunity to find out what they are capable of.

The first spread sets out the rules of a formal debate and the roles of the participants. It uses the issue of 'smacking children' as a vehicle for demonstrating how the debate works. The best way for pupils to learn about the process is to take part in the actual debate, and on page 28 additional arguments for and against the motion 'It should be made illegal for parents to smack their children' can be found. This debate comes around at regular intervals and Parliament has so far rejected demands for an anti-smacking law, although this could change in the near future. You could replace this with a debate on a different topic if you wish.

Page 29 Developing your debating skills

On this page there is an explicit focus on debating skills. Developing an argument is, of course, the central skill involved in debating or any form of discussion. In critical thinking an argument is defined as a statement plus a reason or is sometimes expressed as a reason and a conclusion where the reason supports the conclusion. Since it is the keystone of debates, it is stated explicitly here as 'making points, giving reasons' so that pupils are clear about what an argument is. In Books 2 and 3 the notion of an argument and what constitutes arguing and making a reasoned case for a proposition will be developed progressively around real topics. So it is a good idea if pupils become familiar with the basic statement of an argument and apply it in discussions and debates.

The second area mentioned on page 29 is researching. While it is not a direct debating skill, researching an issue is crucial to any real debate. In many discussions and debates involving pupils, some of them are arguing from a position of ignorance and simply expressing half- or ill-formed opinions. It is essential that they research information about the issue, collect evidence or look at arguments that have been put forward on different sides of the issue before the debate. So we have included research as a necessary adjunct to a formal debate.

This is Citizenship 1 Teacher's Resource Book

Section 1: Rules and fairness, rights and responsibilities

Reflection

Pupil's Book p. 30

Reflection and review of their own learning is important for pupils because it helps them to recognise and value what they have learnt, and to understand the purpose and intended learning outcomes of citizenship education. You will need to assess their learning more formally at specific points within the course, so that you can make a judgement about each pupil's level of attainment at the end of Key Stage 3. However, the pupils' self-assessments can form part of your judgements.

The learning cycle is a good reminder of the processes that reinforce learning through reflection and review.

At the end of an activity, a unit or a module, pupils should reflect on what they did, what happened, who said what and how they feel about all of this. The next stage encourages them to review what they learnt from all of this. What skills and knowledge have they gained? Do they need to improve on their skills and knowledge and, if so, how will they improve? On some occasions, the pupils can be encouraged to apply their new skills and knowledge to other situations, so that there is progression in learning.

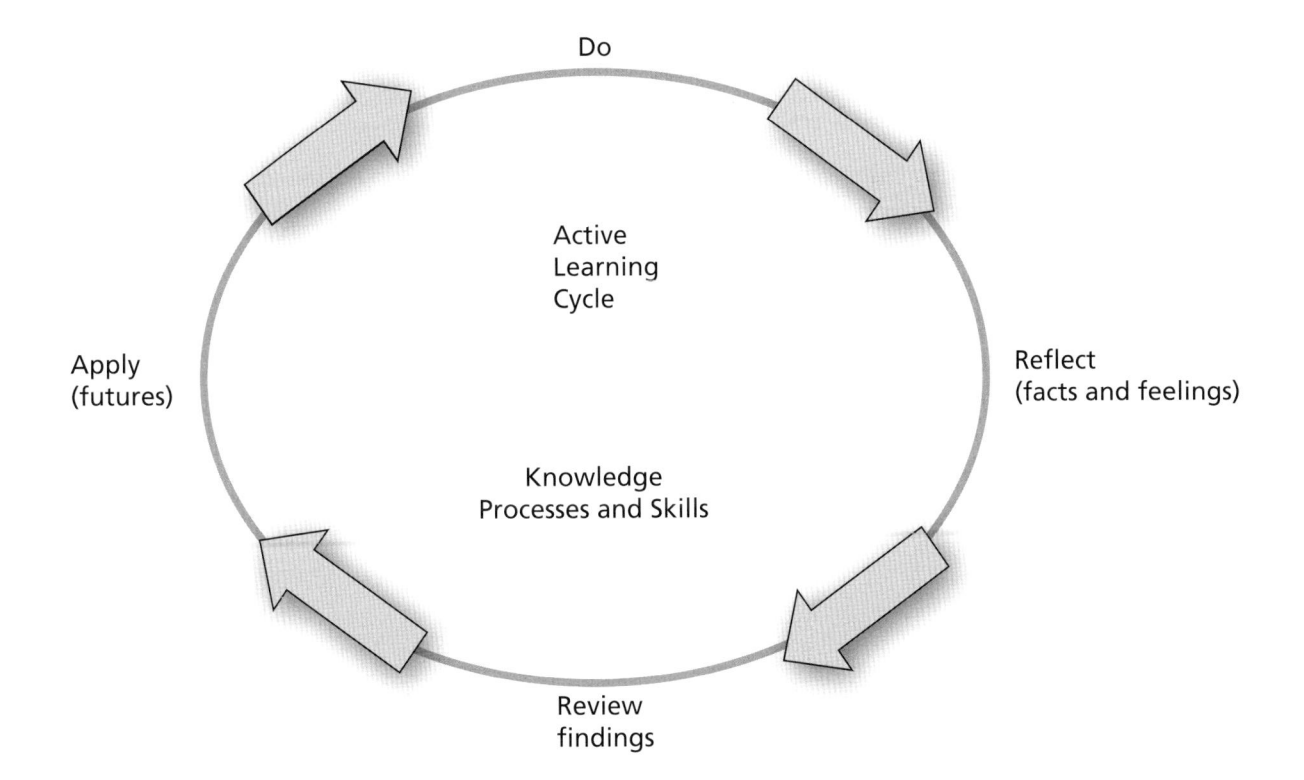

Active Learning Cycle

Do → Reflect (facts and feelings) → Review findings → Apply (futures)

Knowledge Processes and Skills

This is Citizenship 1 Teacher's Resource Book

Activity sheet 1

School rules

School uniform:
- Boys – black jacket, trousers, white shirt, school tie, socks and shoes
- Girls – black jacket, knee-length skirt, flat shoes, white shirt, black tights or white socks
- PE kit as advised

Personal appearance:
- Hair presentable – not highlighted or dyed. Long hair must be tied back for safety and hygiene
- No face make-up
- No jewellery

Equipment:
- Pupils must bring to each lesson pen, pencil, ruler, coloured pencils, rubber, protractor.

Not allowed:
- Personal stereos, mobile phones, audio/video equipment, computer games or skates of any sort

Conduct:
- Every pupil has the right to attend class and take part in activities without other people hindering them.
- Pupils should speak politely to teachers and be treated courteously in return.
- Every person should be treated with dignity.
- Positive or good behaviour will be recognised.
- Bad behaviour will be challenged and pupils so behaving will be isolated from their classmates.
- Pupils may be kept in detention at break and lunchtime, and for 20 minutes after school, without any notice being given.
- Parents will be given 24 hours' notice of longer after-school detentions, usually one hour in length. Friday detention lasts for two hours.

Pupils are expected to:
- aim for 100 per cent attendance
- learn as much as you can
- behave well and treat others in a caring way
- make the most of the learning opportunities offered to you
- recognise the qualities and talents that you have
- try to meet targets and deadlines
- tell staff if you have any problems.

If you were the teacher ...

Use this sheet with the Activity on pages 6–7.

Jenny Bennett's decisions	Right/wrong/ partly right	What you would have done and why
Decision 1 Gave John late detention		
Decision 2 Susan could not go on trip		
Decision 3 Took Jason's phone away		
Decision 4 Did nothing		
Decision 5 Kept whole class in for 15 minutes at lunchtime		
Decision 6 Sent John to deputy head, who told him to go home		
Decision 7 Ignored comments		
Decision 8 Told class essays must be in or they would be dropped from course		

Activity sheet 2

© Hodder Education, 2008 *This is Citizenship 1 Teacher's Resource Book*

Activity sheet 3

Who goes?

Cut out these cards and use them for the Activity on page 10.

A Some pupils worked very hard, but did not produce much work that went into the class folder.	**G** One pupil worked fairly hard on the project and missed a previous school treat because he was very ill. He is better now.
B Two pupils did a lot of the work at home using their parents' computers and colour printers.	**H** A disagreement has been going on for some time between two pupils. An outing together might help them make up.
C One pupil is very unhappy at the moment because of problems at home and it would really cheer her up.	**I** The mother of one of the pupils was very interested in the competition and came in to class to help out.
D Several pupils do not have smart school uniforms.	**J** Two pupils have done a lot of excellent work, as usual. They have won prizes before because they are very clever.
E A group of pupils did a lot of work, but they have been misbehaving in some of their other lessons and are on report.	**K** One pupil, who has produced some good work, suffers badly from asthma and might be ill if she gets too excited.
F Three pupils came to see you privately and begged to be allowed to go because they want to be on television.	**L** It would be good to have equal numbers of boys and girls.

This is Citizenship 1 Teacher's Resource Book © Hodder Education, 2008

Activity sheet 4

What is the fairest way to give pupils places in secondary schools?

Use with the Activity on page 13. Some examples have been put in to help you get started.

Method	Arguments for	Arguments against
Lottery	Fairer – everybody gets an equal chance. No way for parents or teachers to manipulate system.	Pupils might not get into school near them – may have to travel miles
Distance to school		Richer parents buy houses near school – not fair
Catchment area		
Ability		
Siblings		
Faith		

© Hodder Education, 2008 *This is Citizenship 1 Teacher's Resource Book*

Activity sheet 5

How would you like to be treated?

Use this sheet before starting the Activity on page 14.

Writing a charter

Work in fours. You are going to write a charter about how all children should be treated.

1 Split into pairs. Under each of the following headings, make three points about how you would like to be treated and, therefore, how every child should be treated.
   - In school, by teachers
   - In town, by the police, bus drivers, shopkeepers
   - In the home, by your family and carers
   - Out of school and in the playground, by other children
2 Join up with the other pair. Compare your lists of points. Agree which points you will put in your charter.
3 Write your charter on to a poster. Illustrate it and pin it on the wall. Look at the other posters and see where they agree and disagree with your poster.

A charter for children

Activity sheet 6

What rights should all children have?

Use this sheet for question 2 of the Activity on page 14. Write down the rights that children should have.

It is important that children should have the right to ...	It is not very important that children should have the right to ...	Children should NOT have the right to ...
Free education		

© Hodder Education, 2008 *This is Citizenship 1 Teacher's Resource Book*

Activity sheet 7

Quiz

1 There is broken glass under the swings in the local park. You realise that small children could be hurt. Do you:
   a) avoid the glass yourself and do nothing?
   b) find an adult who works in the park and tell them?
   c) pick up the glass and put it in the bin?
   d) do something else?

2 You know that there is a bullying problem in your class. You are not involved yourself, but you know what is going on and you don't like it. Do you:
   a) ignore it because it's none of your business?
   b) tell the class teacher who the bullies are?
   c) raise the general topic of bullying during tutorial and discuss a class strategy to deal with it?
   d) do something else?

3 There are lots of old people living on your estate. Some of them seem quite frightened of young people, like you and your friends. Do you:
   a) feel bad, but do nothing?
   b) talk to them occasionally, in a friendly way, so they don't feel threatened?
   c) suggest to the local day centre that they organise some regular meetings for old and young people to meet and talk?
   d) do something else?

4 Someone has written some racist graffiti on a wall near your school. Do you:
   a) ignore it – it's offensive, but there's nothing you can do?
   b) wash the graffiti off yourself or scribble over it?
   c) complain to the local council and ask for it to be removed?
   d) do something else?

5 You have been learning about the problem of waste and rubbish, and you think more people should recycle their glass, tins, paper, plastic, etc. The school grounds are full of such litter. Do you:
   a) do nothing – it's not your responsibility?
   b) take your own litter to the recycling bins?
   c) suggest to the school council that it campaigns for recycling bins in school to stop litter-dropping?
   d) do something else?

6 An article in your local newspaper reports wrongly on an incident that happened in your school and puts the school in a bad light. Do you:
   a) get cross, but do nothing?
   b) email or write to the paper to complain?
   c) start a petition in the school to support a letter requesting that the newspaper prints an apology?
   d) do something else?

7 You are concerned about child labour in other parts of the world and have done a project on it in school. Do you:
   a) give your project in to your teacher and do nothing else?
   b) decide to boycott certain goods which may have been made by children?
   c) help produce an exhibition on child labour and ask that it be displayed in the school, to tell others about it?
   d) do something else?

8 You are not happy with the way that the school council works. It doesn't seem to get anything done. Do you:
   a) have nothing to do with the school council?
   b) stand as the class representative yourself?
   c) persuade the council to have an open meeting at which criticisms can be discussed?
   d) do something else?

This is Citizenship 1 Teacher's Resource Book © Hodder Education, 2008

Activity sheet 8

Assertive behaviour

Assertiveness means:

- believing in yourself
- recognising that you have rights and so do other people
- respecting all other people, even if you do not like or agree with them
- being sensitive to other people's feelings
- not putting other people down
- being calm and in control of yourself
- being clear about what you want to happen
- recognising that you make mistakes, and learning from them
- accepting responsibility for your own actions
- being honest.

Most people do not like to say 'no' to teachers, friends, family or employers. Sometimes, because of conflicting responsibilities, we have to. Here are some tips on being assertive when saying 'no':

- Be clear and firm without being abrupt – don't stutter and mumble.
- Do not over-apologise or give lots of different reasons. One or two real reasons will do. Don't make up excuses. Be honest.
- Look the other person in the eye.
- If you can't refuse the request, say why it causes you problems and try negotiating.

Activity

1 Think of three situations when you have not behaved very assertively. List each one in column 1. (Continue the chart overleaf if you need more space to write.)
2 In column 2, write down how you behaved at the time.
3 In column 3, say how you could behave more assertively next time.

Situation	How I behaved	How I could behave more assertively in future

© Hodder Education, 2008 *This is Citizenship 1 Teacher's Resource Book*

Activity sheet 9

Being passive, aggressive or assertive

Many people find it very hard to behave calmly, firmly and fairly in difficult situations.

Sometimes people put up with things, even though they are not happy with the situation. They say nothing because they want to avoid arguments or disagreements with other people. This is called **passive** behaviour.

Other people get very angry, shout or swear. They refuse to accept that someone else may have a point of view. This is called **aggressive** behaviour.

Assertive behaviour means that you listen to what other people say and try to find out the truth. You then calmly explain your side of things and say what you want to happen.

Activity 1

Look at the situation in this box and answer questions 1 and 2.

Situation
A teacher sees you out of class when you are taking a message to the office. Without waiting for an explanation, the teacher assumes you are skipping your lesson and starts to tell you off. You have been known to truant in the past.

1 Would you:
- ☐ A interrupt the teacher and shout that you are taking a message and then walk away
- ☐ B say nothing but feel embarrassed and very angry
- ☐ C wait for the teacher to finish and then explain where you are going, showing him/her the message?

Put a tick (3) in one of the boxes.

2 Look again at **A**, **B** and **C**. Which behaviour is passive, which is aggressive and which is assertive?

A is _____ .

B is _____ .

C is _____ .

This is Citizenship 1 Teacher's Resource Book © Hodder Education, 2008

Activity sheet 9 (continued)

Activity 2

For each of the following situations, write three sentences describing
a) a passive response, **b)** an aggressive response and **c)** an assertive response.

1 You have bought a T-shirt from a market stall and you find a hole in it when you get home.
   a) _____
   b) _____
   c) _____

2 A school friend has promised to return a computer game he borrowed from you but forgets to bring it to school several times.
   a) _____
   b) _____
   c) _____

3 Your sister borrows your Walkman without asking you.
   a) _____
   b) _____
   c) _____

4 A friend tells you that someone in the school has been spreading rumours about you.
   a) _____
   b) _____
   c) _____

5 Your best friend has agreed to go to the cinema with you on Saturday, but rings at the last minute to say she is going shopping with another friend.
   a) _____
   b) _____
   c) _____

© Hodder Education, 2008 *This is Citizenship 1 Teacher's Resource Book*

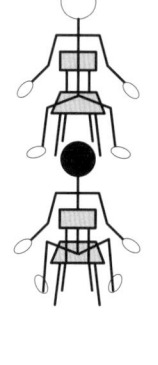

Activity sheet 10A

Practising saying 'no' assertively

It is often difficult to say 'no' to requests even when you know you should. This Activity will give you practice in refusing requests assertively.

1 Arrange the chairs in a large room in two circles, one inside the other. The inner and outer chairs should face each other. If there are more than twenty pupils in the class, you may need to have two sets of circles.
2 Each pupil sitting in the outer circle, facing inwards, should ask the pupil opposite the question on the slip of paper given by the teacher. The pupil sitting opposite in the inner circle, facing outwards, should refuse the request assertively.
3 The person asking may try to wheedle, beg or bully to persuade the other person to agree to the request. However, the person being asked should assertively say 'no'.
4 After three minutes, everyone sitting in the outer circle should move one seat to the right and ask the new partner opposite the same question.
5 The activity continues until people in the outer circle have been right round and asked everyone in the inner circle the same question.
6 When everyone has had a go, pupils sitting in the inner circle should swap with pupils sitting in the outer circle. Repeat the activity.

At the end, think about:

- the different ways people tried to make the person opposite say 'yes'
- how difficult it was to keep saying 'no'
- whether anyone gave in
- whether anyone became aggressive.

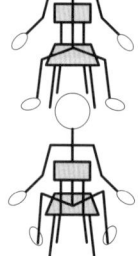

Questions for Activity sheet 10A

Cut up the questions and give one to each pupil in the outer circle. Each pupil in the outer circle must have a different question, so that, as the outer circle moves round, each pupil in the inner circle has to answer a different question.

Can I copy your homework?	Will you look after my little sister on Thursday?
Will you come with me to the cinema?	Will you tell the teacher that I am ill and can't come to school?
Can I borrow your watch?	Will you lend me your revision notes the night before the geography exam?
Will you come to a party at my house at the weekend?	Can I tell my mum I am staying at your house on Saturday night, even though I won't be?
Can I bring a friend round to your house this evening to listen to music?	Will you lend me £5?

Activity sheet 11

Dealing with criticism

Nobody likes to be criticised. Criticism makes us feel bad about ourselves and bad about the person who made the criticism. A passive response to criticism is to believe it, whether it is true or not. This can make a person feel very bad.

An aggressive response to criticism is to believe none of it and to be hostile to the person who is being critical.

However, sometimes criticism can help us to change for the better if the criticism is made carefully and thoughtfully and if we learn how to deal with it assertively. To deal with criticism assertively, you should do the following:

- Listen to *what* is being said rather than *how* it is said.
- Consider whether any of the criticism is true and decide whether you agree with it.
- Decide how to reply calmly, agreeing or disagreeing where necessary.
- Make any change to your behaviour that you think is required.

Activity

1 In pairs, talk about times you have been criticised. Try to think of one example where the criticism was fair and one example where it was unfair.
2 For each example, act out an assertive response with your partner.
3 Discuss your examples with the whole class.
4 Some of the pairs could role-play their assertive responses.

This is Citizenship 1 Teacher's Resource Book © Hodder Education, 2008

Section 2: Communities and identities

Aim of section

In this section, pupils consider what it means to be part of a community and how membership of different communities can influence a person's identity. It is a central part of citizenship education for young people to understand that all members of society, including themselves, learn their values, beliefs and attitudes from the various influences upon them. However, it is also important that they recognise that individuals interpret these influences differently, and that people should not be stereotyped by any of their characteristics, whether these are age, ethnicity, religion or anything else. The section introduces pupils to the differing meanings of the word 'community' and to the range of influences that might have contributed to their own sense of identity.

The second part of the section encourages pupils to think about what they like and do not like about their own communities, what could be changed and how change could be achieved. At this point they are introduced to the idea of 'active citizenship': the part that all members of communities can play in improving people's lives and circumstances. The role of local government in such improvement is examined in Book 2, but pupils may begin to consider local politics during their discussion of these issues. The section also introduces some of the tensions that occur within communities – we deal here with age, and the seemingly increasing gap between the young and the old. Other tensions – ethnic, religious, class – are examined in Books 2 and 3. The section ends with an activity that aims to build community cohesion – the development of a community website.

CITIZENSHIP PROGRAMME OF STUDY

This section covers the following concepts and processes:

Key concepts

1.1 Democracy and justice

c. Considering how democracy, justice, diversity, toleration, respect and freedom are valued by people with different beliefs, backgrounds and traditions within a changing democratic society

1.2 Rights and responsibilities

c. Investigating ways in which rights can compete and conflict, and understanding that hard decisions have to be made to try to balance these

1.3 Identities and diversity: living together in the UK

a. Appreciating that identities are complex, can change over time and are informed by different understandings of what it means to be a citizen in the UK

b. Exploring the diverse national, regional, ethnic and religious cultures, groups and communities in the UK and the connections between them

d. Exploring community cohesion

Key processes

2.1 Critical thinking and enquiry

Pupils should be able to:

a. engage with and reflect on different ideas, opinions, beliefs and values when exploring topical and controversial issues and problems

b. research, plan and undertake enquiries into issues and problems

2.2 Advocacy and representation

Pupils should be able to:

a. express and explain their own opinions to others through discussions

b. communicate an argument, taking account of different viewpoints and drawing on what they have learnt through research, action and debate

2.3 Taking informed and responsible action

Pupils should be able to:

a. explore creative approaches to taking action on problems and issues to achieve intended purposes

b. analyse the impact of their actions on communities

c. reflect on the progress they have made

Section 2: Communities and identities

2.1 Belonging to a community

Pupil's Book pp. 32–33

In this spread, the idea of 'community' is explored through three examples of different young people, and the various groups they belong to. Pupils are then asked to identify those communities that they themselves belong to.

The word 'community' is used in many different ways in everyday speech, and often causes confusion. It might help to try to clarify the different meanings of 'community' at the start of the section. Ask everyone in the class to make up a sentence that contains the word 'community' and to write the sentence on a strip of paper. Alternatively, you could ask them to write a sentence beginning: 'A community is . . .'

When pupils are asked, in question 3, to list different types of communities, the following are likely to occur:

- a number of people living in the same geographical area who may not know each other
- people living near each other who all do the same work (for example, a farming community)
- an organised group who know each other and meet regularly (for example, at a club or a place of worship)
- a group of people having the same religion, ethnic group, race
- a group of people who meet regularly because they have a common interest (for example, drama or sport)

Work with the pupils to come to a definition of community that includes the following features:

- a sense of a common bond with other people
- feeling an obligation to these people
- sharing aspects of identity and having some things in common
- agreeing about the importance of something.

The Scouts are discussed on this spread as an example of a community working at different levels – local, national and global – and it is one which involves young people in a range of activities around common interests. It is also an organisation that has changed dramatically from its early days when it existed only for boys and promoted Christianity. It now celebrates the diversity of young Scouts and encourages international understanding and active citizenship. You could ask pupils to further research the philosophy of the Scouts or to find other organisations with similar aims, for example Woodcraft Folk.

2.2 Identities

Pupil's Book pp. 34–41
Activity sheets 12, 13

The first spread in this subsection enables pupils to explore the various influences on their *cultural* identity. A definition of culture is provided, since it is important, as part of citizenship studies, to encourage pupils to focus on cultural features such as traditions, religious beliefs, values, food and clothing, rather than personality characteristics, which might form a slightly different aspect of their identity. Pupils are asked to select those influences illustrated on the spread that have had the greatest impact on their own identity (see Pupil's Book, pages 34–35). You will need to clarify what we mean by 'cultural identity', helping pupils to distinguish between those parts of identity which arise from origins, traditions, beliefs, etc., and a 'sense of self', which includes things like personality traits, strengths and weaknesses, self-esteem, etc. Some influences, which appear not to be cultural, might be. For example, sports team loyalty may be based on region, class or even religion, as may be illustrated by the Rangers/Celtic situation in Scotland. Other influences, such as hobbies and interests, music tastes and fashion, can arise from current-day youth culture.

Section 2: Communities and identities

As you explain this task, you could strengthen pupils' understanding of the importance of some of these features to different people by citing examples such as

- family – the Mitchells in *EastEnders*
- where I live – 'maybe it's because I'm a Londoner ...'
- place of birth – 'the green, green grass of home'.

When the class starts working on the task, you can go around the class and, sensitively, choose examples from the pupils' work to present to the rest of the class. This will generate more ideas and so build a fuller understanding.

You could use a card sort to carry out the task, using the cards cut up from **Activity sheet 12**. Ask pupils to spread the cards out on the table and select the ones that are most important to forming their idea of their own identity, i.e. how they see themselves. It is helpful to do this in pairs as the pair can discuss what they understand by each influence and also think about how it might apply to each of them.

The **Activity** on page 35, based on one used in Bishop's Hatfield Girls' School in Hatfield, provides pupils with the opportunity to make a collage expressing their own identity. The real examples provided on pages 36–37 could be discussed before they start. What clues are there in each collage to help us understand how that individual sees his or her own cultural identity?

Once pupils have finished their own collages, these should all be displayed and discussed. The important learning from this Activity is for everyone to appreciate how individuals interpret the wide range of influences upon them, and make choices for themselves. It would also be interesting to look back at the influences illustrated on pages 34–35, to see how many of these are illustrated and how many are shared within the class.

Pages 38–41 Different identities

On these two spreads there are a number of short interviews with real young people who describe what is important to them and how their different identities impact on their lives. The point to stress here is that we all have multiple identities, which influence us differently depending on the context we are in. It is suggested that pupils interview each other and write up their own case studies. All people have a cultural identity, white English as much as any other group, and this **Activity** enables them to recognise their own. They could use **Activity sheet 13** to help them carry out the interviews.

Finally, in this subsection, pupils discuss the ways in which differing cultural identities manifest themselves in communities. The illustration on page 41 shows different food shops, places of worship, clothing and behaviour. Pupils should identify evidence of aspects of different cultures from the picture. It is important to note that keeping a dog as a pet, carrying a handbag and using a skateboard are also aspects of cultural behaviour, in addition to the seemingly more obvious features such as eating halal food and worshipping at a synagogue. As a follow-up activity, your own pupils may wish to visit their local high street and make a note of evidence of different cultures. In some parts of the country, there may be little obvious evidence of cultural diversity. In this situation, pupils should be encouraged to look out for examples of traditions and customs from different sub-cultural groups: Europeans who are not British (Italian restaurants, Polish food shops), services for second-home owners (gardening and house-sitting offered), differences between behaviour and interests of elderly inhabitants and local youth (different clothing, day centres for the elderly, graffiti), perhaps even social class differences (bingo or field sports suppliers – hunting, shooting and fishing). It has been said that many young Britons do not recognise their own culture, as a fish does not recognise the water it swims in. This activity can raise awareness that we all belong to cultures and sub-cultures, and that these influence our attitudes and behaviour.

This is Citizenship 1 Teacher's Resource Book

Section 2: Communities and identities

2.3 Living together in communities

Pupil's Book pp. 42–45
Activity sheet 14

In these spreads, the idea of potential conflict in communities is introduced. In this book we use age as an illustration because young people can unite in their view that they are sometimes stereotyped by older people, and that they in turn stereotype the elderly.

Stereotypes are descriptions of groups of people who have something in common, such as their religion, age, sex, nationality or ethnicity. The description is applied to everyone in the group and ignores individual differences between people. The problem for pupils in understanding stereotypes is that groups of people do share some characteristics and therefore pupils may see the stereotypes as accurate in certain respects. But this is quite different from attributing the same characteristics, values and attitudes to everybody in a particular group and ignoring the all-important differences between individuals. This is why stereotypes are dangerous and can lead to prejudice and discrimination. The previous activities should have stressed the importance of individual differences.

The stereotype of age is used here because young people are likely to recognise how inaccurate such stereotypes are when applied to themselves. The words included are often used to describe young people and elderly people. Racist, ethnic and religious stereotypes have not been included, as publishing such words in a school textbook can be seen as legitimising them. However, it is possible during this subsection that issues of ethnicity, race and religion will be raised. Clearly these issues need to be dealt with sensitively, but they should not be ignored or shied away from. It is for you to make a professional judgement about whether to confront extreme stereotypes, such as those used in anti-semitic Nazi propaganda or topical newspaper stories. You could also draw on pupils' own experiences of being ethnically stereotyped. Issues to do with race, ethnicity, gender and disability will be looked at in more depth in Books 2 and 3.

The research task suggests that young people find out more about the views of old and young about each other. It is also a good idea to invite some older people to the class, through Age Concern or a similar organisation, and devise some common task for old and young to work together on. Such intergenerational projects have been successful in breaking down the stereotypes and fears that sometimes exist. You could involve the older visitors in the simulation, Oldthorpe, on pages 43–45. However, it would be best if they took on roles other than 'older residents'.

The simulation involves five groups of people living and working in the town of Oldthorpe. Use **Activity sheet 14** to make copies of the role cards to give out to pupils, and also copies of the proposals. Make sure you allow plenty of time for the various stages set out in the Pupil's Book.

When you run a simulation, it is important to allow adequate time to debrief it (at least one third of the total time). Make sure that you get everyone to stay in role for the first part of the debrief so that they can discuss what happened during the simulation. This is the 'reflection' part of the **Activity**. At the next stage of the debrief, ask the pupils to come out of role. This is often best done by moving their position. Change the seating to a circle, or ask them to change seats with someone else. They should now review what they have learnt about the relationships between old and young.

The best way of extending this role play would be to pick up real local issues – developments or conflicts that are currently taking place – and bring in some of the interest groups involved to engage pupils in the debate about what should happen.

This is Citizenship 1 Teacher's Resource Book

Section 2: Communities and identities

2.4 How would you change your local town centre?

Pupil's Book pp. 46–49
Activity sheets 15, 16

This double-page illustration is designed to provide a way of looking at the local town centre that is accessible to all pupils. Indeed, this illustration could be extremely useful for vocabulary work and language development for ESL pupils and recent arrivals to this country. The main aim here, however, is to encourage pupils to make some assessment of what is good or bad about town centres in general, using this composite image to stimulate thought and discussion. A copy of this illustration is provided on **Activity sheet 15** so that you can reproduce it. Pupils can annotate the sheet in any way you want, for example for language purposes, highlighting good and bad points, etc.

We have used the town centre as we feel the vast majority of pupils will have a town centre which they can relate to, whether in a town or a city (the local high street). Pupils who live in rural areas will also have one town centre which they visit more regularly than others or it could be a large village. An organised visit to the town centre would be extremely advantageous so pupils can make their own notes and drawings, take photographs (using digital cameras) and conduct surveys about the attitudes of the town-centre users. **Activity sheet 16** is a reprint of the survey printed on page 49. The **Activity** on page 48 is designed to help pupils start to develop their research skills, an important aspect of citizenship education. Canvassing the views of citizens to find out what they think about various issues is an important strand of research in citizenship. This and other aspects of researching (using books, the internet, etc.) will be developed further in Books 2 and 3.

After the visit, pupils will have a huge amount of information and stimulating material to consider and assess. This should help them raise their own questions and enquiries about the nature of the town centre, its good and bad points, and how it could be made a more pleasant place to live. The aim here is to get them to engage with the idea that people can play an active role as citizens in bringing about changes that make the places they live better. This would be a suitable moment to bring in councillors or other local interest groups (town society, local historians, tradespeople, environmentalists) to talk to the class. The visit could also lead to work in other areas of the curriculum, for example:

- English – writing letters, making notes, writing descriptions and reports
- geography – survey work, showing data in different forms and interpreting it
- history – local history of the development of the area.

2.5 Are you a good or an active citizen?

Pupil's Book pp. 50–51
Activity sheets 17, 18

There is some confusion about the word 'citizenship', certainly among pupils, but also in the general population.

- Some people think it just refers to the legal status of nationality (i.e. being a British citizen).
- Some people think it means knowing how to behave properly – being a 'good citizen'.
- Some people see it as understanding what it means to be an active member of a democracy.

The aim of citizenship education, as defined by the Crick report (*Education for Citizenship and the Teaching of Democracy in Schools*, QCA, 1998), Ofsted and QCA, is to encourage pupils both to know about our democratic political system and also to learn the skills necessary to take responsible action to bring about democratic change.

This is Citizenship 1 Teacher's Resource Book

Section 2: Communities and identities

This is often referred to as 'active citizenship'.

In this spread, pupils are encouraged to think about the difference between being a 'good citizen' and being an 'active citizen'. The difference is important. It is perfectly possible to be a good citizen while living in a non-democratic country – as long as you obey the law and behave well towards others, you will be left in peace. However, the whole point about living in a democracy is that people can make choices about their leaders, can disagree, can legally protest about things they don't like and can organise to change things. All of this is possible while still being a good citizen, but you also have to be active.

We use the notion of 'active' citizen on this spread to encourage pupils to be *active*. The authors of this book believe that, whatever else citizenship is, it is about participation and people taking an active role in their communities and in national affairs, at least to the extent of voting and taking an interest in such matters.

You might find this a more effective exercise to do as a card sort. The 25 statements in the spread can be sorted in piles: 'good citizen', 'active citizen', 'both good and active citizen'. They can be copied from **Activity sheet 17** and cut up, so that each small group has a set. At the end of the Activity, find out which of the statements were most commonly sorted in each of the piles. Discuss with the pupils the difference between being a 'good' and an 'active citizen'. Ask them to consider which they are and their reasons.

An alternative approach is to pose the question 'What is a good citizen?' and ask the pupils to sort the statements into three piles: agree, disagree and can't decide. This will promote discussion of what a 'good' citizen is and then you can move into the discussion of how this might be different from an 'active' citizen.

For pupils who are interested in active citizenship in a democracy, use **Activity sheet 18**, which lists democratic rights and asks pupils to put them in order of importance to them. Some of the rights might not be available to all, and this could be discussed.

2.6 Can you change anything?

Pupil's Book pp. 52–55
Activity sheet 19

Many people feel powerless when things are happening in their own community that they don't approve of or that adversely affect their lives. This may be to do with the way people around them are behaving, or when decisions by the council seem to have been made without consulting them. This subsection looks at the ways in which people can complain or take action in the local community. Judging what sort of action is appropriate is an important element of citizenship. You could ask pairs of pupils to focus on one or two of the issues, and then join up with another pair that looked at the same issues.

As part of the plenary discussion, you could also raise questions about where the boundaries lie between legal and illegal action. The use of direct action, for example mothers with babies halting cars on a dangerous crossing or animal rights activists attacking hunters, is a growing phenomenon and is a relevant and suitable subject for debate in the classroom. Would they say there are ever arguments for breaking the law to make a point?

Pages 54–55 Being an active citizen

Making a positive change is something that everyone can do. On page 54, there are some suggested issues that pupils could plan to take action on. The idea here is that they use the action plan to think about the way they would go about identifying and investigating an issue and then taking action to bring about a change. This starts them thinking about the process of being an active citizen. In this case they would not fill out the reflection section of the 'Action plan' box. **Activity sheet 19** provides a copy of the action plan that can be photocopied.

Section 2: Communities and identities

However, it would be much more effective if they chose a local issue on their own to investigate. This might be something they identified in their work on town centres. Or it might be something they identify in the neighbourhood around the school. They could then research and carry out some form of action, for instance drawing up some proposals for change that could be sent off to the council. It might be possible to get a councillor to visit to discuss the issue with them. At the end of this pupils could fill out the reflection section of the 'Action Plan' box and think about what they have learnt and what skills they have developed.

2.7 How can we make our communities sustainable?

Pupil's Book pp. 56–59
Activity sheet 20

A number of reports have highlighted the negative impact that landfill sites have on the environment and people who live near them. Landfill is also extremely expensive for councils to use. Similarly, the public is taking direct action to prevent incinerators being opened up near residential areas. So the main debate, especially in relation to sustainability, has moved to the best ways of cutting down waste. It is a huge citizenship issue because it involves government (European Union targets) and local councils but also the actions of private individuals who can act to reduce the amount of waste they produce.

The first spread introduces the topic and then focuses on reducing and reusing waste. **Activity sheet 20** provides a chart that could be used with the main **Activity** on page 57. There is a huge amount of information on the internet about this topic. Probably the most coherent and comprehensive coverage is provided by Waste Watch, which has a website and a helpline to tell the public about how they can recycle all types of materials safely and efficiently (see the 'Resources' section on page 72). The school itself is a good place to start initiatives on recycling and many schools have their own waste programmes in operation.

Page 58 Recycling

This page looks at some of the ideas that have been suggested for encouraging people to recycle. These come up on the new media regularly so you might be able to include the current idea. Charging for waste with electronic chips in bins (some councils are already doing it) seems to be a highly likely option but other schemes have been suggested. Most of these have downsides (for example, fly tipping, putting waste in other people's bins), so there is going to be a continuing debate over the next few years.

Page 59 Campaigning

The last **Activity** asks pupils to plan a campaign, or they could simply produce a poster/leaflet for school. This author is incensed by the distribution of free newspapers which, apart from the fact that they contain little news, is a huge waste of paper and source of litter. So perhaps your pupils would like to take this up, or alternatively the amount of packaging in supermarkets.

2.8 Bringing communities together

Pupil's Book pp. 60–61

Many towns and villages have developed their own webpages. This can promote community cohesion if all members of the local community are included in the activity. Here pupils are encouraged to look at some of these as a lead in to the extended **Activity** on page 61.

Page 61 Make your own community webpage

Pupils are invited to design a webpage for their community, whether it is a village,

Section 2: Communities and identities

borough or small town. The **Activity** enables them to take on different roles (journalists, editors, designers) and each will need support from specialist staff or from members of the local community. It could be a joint project with ICT and/or English. It will probably require support from an IT specialist. If the IT side is too difficult, pupils could still produce their ideas for the website on paper and draw it up as a screen grab from a website. For this project to be successful, pupils will need to carry out research about the local area. The local newspaper office, the local council and the library would be good places to start.

Reflection

As in Section 1, we have provided some suggestions for ways in which pupils can assess their own learning and progress during the section. Pupils can rate their own skills levels using the chart provided in the Pupil's Book, but should try to provide evidence to back up their score and suggestions for improvement. The understanding is checked through sentence completion, short answers and peer review. See the notes in this Teacher's Resource Book for Section 1 (on pages 8–9).

Activity sheet 12

Identities

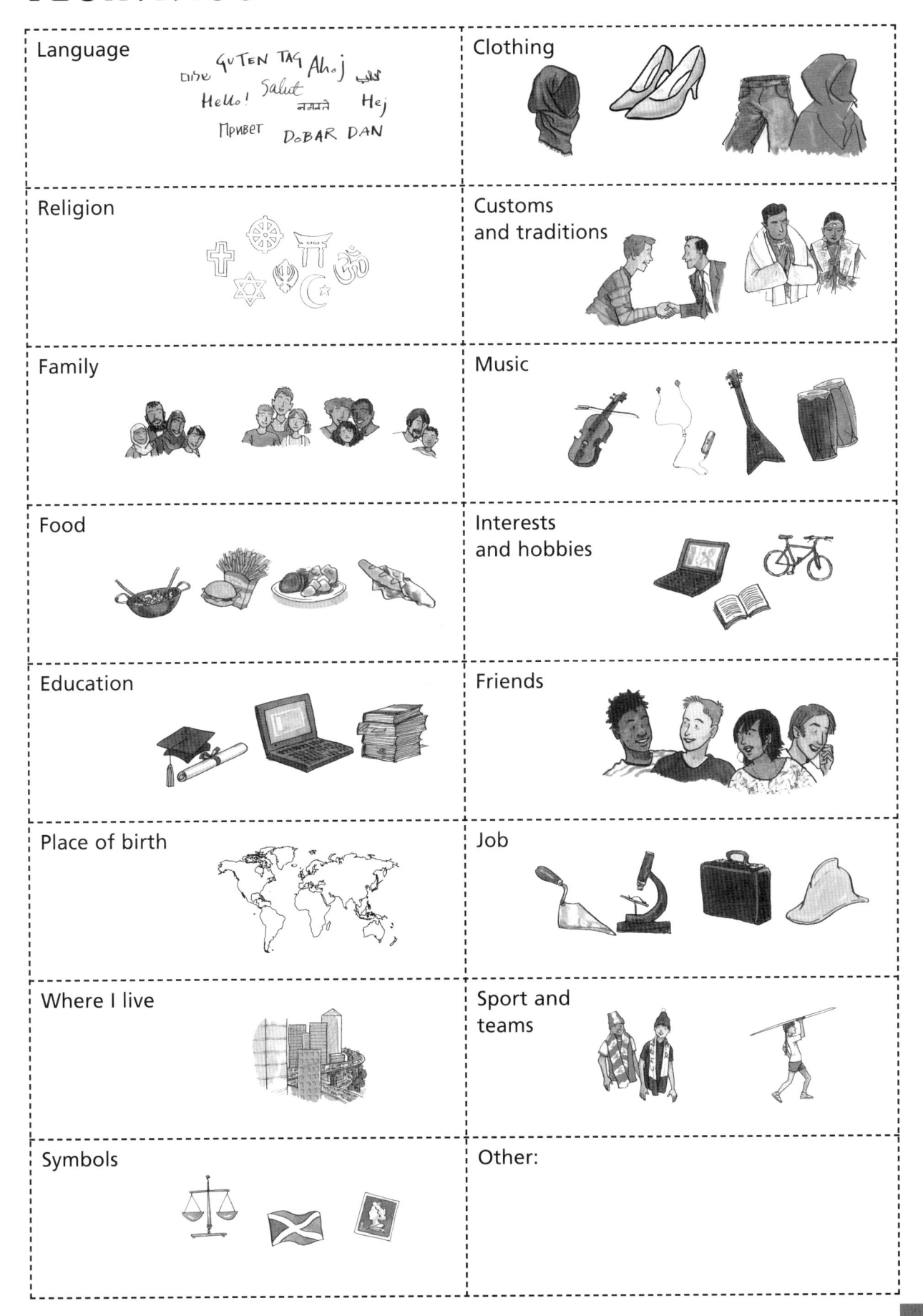

Language	Clothing
Religion	Customs and traditions
Family	Music
Food	Interests and hobbies
Education	Friends
Place of birth	Job
Where I live	Sport and teams
Symbols	Other:

© Hodder Education, 2008 *This is Citizenship 1 Teacher's Resource Book*

Activity sheet 13

Interview

Work in pairs and interview each other about your identity.
You could choose from the following questions and keep a note of what your interviewee says in the boxes.

1 What would you say are the most important influences on your own cultural identity?

2 Have you always lived in this area? If not, where else have you lived? What influences do the areas you have lived in have on you?

3 What sports teams do you support and why? How important are these to you?

4 What traditions do you and your family always follow?

5 How important are friends to your identity? What interests do you share with them?

Activity sheet 14

Oldthorpe

Cut out these cards and give them to the members of the relevant group.

Older residents

You have lived and worked in Oldthorpe all your lives. It used to be a safe place – people knew each other, because most of them worked in the big car plants. Some worked on the production lines and others worked in the offices. You are not happy with the way things are now. New families have come to your town to live in the modern estates that have been built on the outskirts. They often travel into the neighbouring town to work, so people don't know each other as well as they used to. The children from these families seem out of order and unruly. There has been some vandalism, and one of your friends was insulted and threatened. The children gather in large groups in the shopping centre, so you tend not to go there any more.

What do you think could make the situation better?

Young people

Some of you were born in Oldthorpe and some came to live here when you were babies. It's your town. You have grown up here and go to school here. This is where your friends are. There is very little to do. You are too young to go into pubs, and there is very little else to amuse young people. Your parents worry about you going off into the surrounding countryside. You are always being moved on from the shopping centre, and you are accused of scaring off older people, so occasionally the police have been called.

What do you think could make the situation better?

Local councillors

You are elected members of the local council and it is your job to make sure Oldthorpe is a safe, clean and happy place for people to live. You know there's a problem at the shopping centre, where groups of young people hang around and often get moved on by the security staff. The police are sometimes called when there is trouble. You could fund some proposals to improve the situation. It seems that the older residents are frightened of the youth, and the youth feel picked on.

What do you think could make the situation better?

© Hodder Education, 2008 *This is Citizenship 1 Teacher's Resource Book*

Activity sheet 14 (continued)

The police

You are senior police officers in Oldthorpe and, if something is not done about the relationship between the old and young, you can see real trouble looming in the town. Older people feel that the young have taken over the shopping centre and other parts of the town, and they are frightened to walk the streets. Your officers sometimes get called when there is trouble, but you don't want to make things worse by arresting anyone. This could create a great deal of hostility. The Community Support Officers sometimes patrol the shopping centre, but you do not think that the problem is really one that can be solved by the police.

What do you think could make the situation better?

Shopping centre manager and staff

You are responsible for the running of the Oldthorpe shopping centre and for the safety of all customers. There are seats and coffee bars in the centre that have been attracting groups of young people. They are noisy, but they seem pretty harmless. They spend some money in the music shops, clothes shops and cafés, so some of the shopkeepers don't mind them being there. However, you get many complaints from other customers because they are scared of the youth, and some of them say they won't come to the centre any more.

What do you think could make the situation better?

Proposals

There are many proposals that have been put to the local council to try to solve the problem. They include:

- opening more youth centres in the town
- opening more day care and activity centres for the elderly
- making some areas of the town (parts of parks) for old people only and other areas purely for young people (recreation areas)
- running regular events (festivals, carnivals) when old and young can mix and get to know each other
- appointing more Community Support Officers to help the security staff control the youth
- banning young people in groups of more than three from entering the shopping centre
- inviting older people to talk to the young people at school, and to work with them on projects to improve the town.

This is Citizenship 1 Teacher's Resource Book © Hodder Education, 2008

Activity sheet 15

Town centre

35

Activity sheet 16

Survey

SURVEY ON _____ CENTRE [insert name of town]		
Would you mind helping us find out what people in this area think of _____?		
We are carrying out some research into people's views on the good and bad points of our local centre, and would be grateful for a few moments of your time.		
1 Do you live in this area? 2 Do you work in the area? 3 Are you a visitor to the area?	Yes/No Yes/No Yes/No	
4 Which of the following do you like about the town?	Cleanliness Attractive buildings Car parking Shops Restaurants and bars Parks Safety Entertainment facilities Transport Facilities for all ages Friendliness of local people Other: [say what] _____	☐ [tick] ☐ ☐ ☐ ☐ ☐ ☐ ☐ ☐ ☐ ☐ ☐
5 Which of the following do you *not* like about the town?	Litter and graffiti Buildings Types of shops Lack of parks and green areas Restaurants and bars Feels unsafe No parking Busy roads Infrequent transport Lack of facilities for all ages Unfriendliness of local people Other: [say what] _____	☐ [tick] ☐ ☐ ☐ ☐ ☐ ☐ ☐ ☐ ☐ ☐ ☐
6 Which is the *best* thing about the town?		
7 Which is the *worst* thing about the town?		
8 What needs to be done to make the town better?		
Thank you very much for your time.		

Activity sheet 17

Are you a good or an active citizen?

Use this sheet as an alternative approach to question 1 of the Activity on page 50. The blank boxes can be used to add your own statements if you wish.

A votes in elections to choose who should run the country	B never drops litter on the streets	C takes part in local campaigns, e.g. to oppose a new building or demand a pedestrian crossing
D works for a local charity	E reports neighbours to the local authority if they are noisy	F never has parties, in case the noise disturbs the neighbours
G tells people off for dropping litter or letting their dogs foul the street	H obeys all laws and rules at all times	I stays out late at night having a good time with friends
J takes newspapers and bottles to the recycling centre	K watches the neighbours very closely to make sure they are not up to mischief	L has strong religious beliefs and worships regularly
M takes part in election campaigns by distributing leaflets for a political party	N takes part in protests over important issues (e.g. where a road is being built through a beauty spot), even if this means breaking the law	O does not write graffiti on walls
P reports vandals to the police	Q takes part in a Neighbourhood Watch group to prevent crime	R is pleasant to people if they ask for help (e.g. giving directions)
S takes books back to the library on time	T votes in elections to choose who should run the local council	U helps elderly neighbours and pops round to check they are OK
V does not talk loudly on a mobile phone in a public place	W does not put their feet on the seats of buses and trains	X takes an interest in current affairs and watches the news
Y writes letters to MPs (Members of Parliament) or the local council about things that seem wrong		

© Hodder Education, 2008 *This is Citizenship 1 Teacher's Resource Book*

Activity sheet 18

Active citizenship in a democracy

The following are all rights that people living in a democracy take for granted. Put them in order of importance for you.
  Discuss whether we do in fact have all of these rights.

The right to:

Vote for the people who will govern us

Have a fair trial

Be able to marry whoever we like

Be able to have as many children as we want

Own property such as a house or a business

Travel to anywhere in the world

Belong to any organisation

Protest against laws that we think are unfair

Go on demonstrations

Express our opinions

Disagree with other people

Read any books we choose

Save money

Wear what we like

Read the newspapers we choose to read

Activity sheet 19

Action plan

	Action	Comments
IDENTIFY THE ISSUE What is wrong or needs changing?		
CARRY OUT RESEARCH What information do we need? Where shall we look for information? How will we find out what other people think about this issue? How could things be improved?		
PLAN AND CARRY OUT ACTION What different kinds of action could we take? Who can help us? Who will we work with? What action shall we definitely take?		
REFLECT ON THE ACTION (*Only fill out this section if you have carried out an action*) What worked well? What didn't work well? What should we have done differently? Was the action successful?		

© Hodder Education, 2008 *This is Citizenship 1 Teacher's Resource Book*

Activity sheet 20

Recycling and reducing waste

Use this sheet for the second Activity on page 57.

Complete the chart by explaining how the items could be re-used or reduced. Add other items to the chart.

Product	How to re-use	How to reduce
Clothes	Take to charity shop, hand down to smaller children	Buy fewer clothes, mend clothes so can use longer
Food		
Toys		
Shoes		
Plastic bags		
Glass bottles		
Books		
China		
Computers		
Mobile phones		
Packaging		

This is Citizenship 1 Teacher's Resource Book © Hodder Education, 2008

Section 3: Being a global citizen

Aim of section

This section aims to introduce pupils to some of the issues associated with being part of a global community. The activities help them to think of themselves as global citizens who can play a part in what is going on in the world. The early part of the section is concerned with pupils' images of other countries and what they know about them, particularly if their families originate from outside the UK or if they have relatives who live abroad. This is designed to point up some of the misconceptions that pupils have of 'foreign' places. Then the pupils look at the way they are connected with other countries.

The second part of the section focuses on the economic relations between countries and the social and environmental implications of these relations in respect of trade and tourism. The pupils consider how the actions of people (consumers) in the UK, agencies and governments can have a profound effect on the livelihoods and cultures of people in the developing world. They think about how they, as individuals, might take responsible action to improve the lives of others. This includes our attitudes to and involvement with international charities. The topics are set in a framework of human rights, but this theme will be developed in greater depth in Books 2 and 3.

3.1 What do you know about other countries?

Pupil's Book pp. 64–67
Activity sheet 21

Some pupils in your class are likely to have first-hand knowledge of other countries in the world and they can be used as a resource. The **Activity** on page 64 is designed to establish prior knowledge of other countries and make pupils aware of the complex web of links that exist between their classroom and the rest of the world. It also provides an opportunity to value the diversity that may exist in the class and at

---

> **CITIZENSHIP PROGRAMME OF STUDY**
> This section covers the following concepts and processes:
>
> **Key concepts**
> 1.1 Democracy and justice
> b. Weighing up what is fair and unfair in different situations
> 1.2 Rights and responsibilities
> a. Exploring different kinds of rights and obligations and how these affect both individuals and communities
> c. Investigating ways in which rights can compete and conflict, and understanding that hard decisions have to be made to try to balance these
>
> **Key processes**
> 2.1 Critical thinking and enquiry
> Pupils should be able to:
> a. engage with and reflect on different ideas, opinions, beliefs and values when exploring topical and controversial issues and problems
> b. research, plan and undertake enquiries into issues and problems
> 2.2 Advocacy and representation
> Pupils should be able to:
> a. express and explain their own opinions to others through discussions, formal debates and voting
> b. communicate an argument, taking account of different viewpoints and drawing on what they have learnt through research, action and debate
> d. represent the views of others, with which they may or may not agree
> 2.3 Taking informed and responsible action
> Pupils should be able to:
> a. explore creative approaches to taking action on problems and issues to achieve intended purposes
> b. work individually and with others to negotiate, plan and take action on citizenship issues to try to influence others

Section 3: Being a global citizen

appropriate moments pupils may be given the chance to talk about their or their parents'/grandparents' countries of origin. There will be some pupils in your class who have never travelled abroad and have no relatives abroad either. This (origins/travelling) could be a sensitive issue and you will have to judge how far you want your pupils to talk about these. However, there should be no reason why they cannot show their knowledge of other countries and the lifestyles of the inhabitants. A blank map for use in the Activity appears on **Activity sheet 21**. It would be useful to have a set of atlases available.

The **Discuss** activity on page 65 raises the issue of stereotypes that pupils may have of different countries. Italy, Saudi Arabia, the United States, Ethiopia, India and China are suggested for discussion, but you may wish to change the list and replace them with countries in the news. The stereotype of the United States illustrated here shows a rich, acquisitive nation. It would be helpful to point out that there are a large number of poor people in the United States.

This spread also introduces pupils to the terminology associated with the division of the world into richer and poorer countries. The terms 'underdeveloped', 'developing' and 'Third World' for some imply that the countries thus identified are regarded as inferior compared with the terms 'advanced industrial', 'developed' or 'First World', which imply that countries are more advanced and civilised. Some agencies favour the term 'majority world' or 'countries of the south' as less value-laden. It is important that pupils are familiar with these terms.

It is important to stress that every country has social and economic inequality. In the case of the UK, this has been increasing in the last two decades. The richer northern countries have their own share of problems – pollution, crime, etc. – generated by industrial development and urbanisation. This raises questions about the quality of life. Is it to do with material goods or relationships and sense of community?

Many people prefer a so-called 'simpler' lifestyle away from the pressures and stresses of modern industrial society.

Pages 66–67 Images of developing countries

The two collections of images are used to encourage pupils to think about why we have particular views of other countries. Some children have, for instance, a very negative view of countries in Africa and of the people who live in them because they only see photographs of them in times of crisis, for example during floods or famines when the landscape has been devastated and the people are in great need. This is reflected in Collection A. Collection B reveals a different set of images which show that there is a prosperous side to life in many countries regarded as poor. India, which has the largest number of poor people in the world, is undergoing rapid change and has a fast-growing economy which is generating modern cities with dramatic new buildings. Jobs are being created, many for a burgeoning middle class.

3.2 How are you connected to the world?

Pupil's Book pp. 68–69

This spread seeks to strengthen pupils' understanding of the way they are connected to other parts of the world and how they are exposed to cultural and other influences, some of which are absorbed into their lifestyles. The pupils should work in groups and use large pieces of paper (A3 or even bigger) to give them plenty of space to develop their spider diagrams. The 'food and drink' category is used as an example to show how they might build the diagram. You could encourage them to look at home at manufactured items to see where they originate. The groups could display and explain their charts, prompting a wider discussion of their global interconnections.

Section 3: Being a global citizen

The **Activity** on page 69 is designed to make pupils aware that our lifestyles are predicated on the materials and cheap goods that come from abroad and that cheap mass travel allows many of us to enjoy foreign holidays – globalisation brings many benefits. But there is often a price to be paid for this and pupils are encouraged to think about the disadvantages of globalisation in terms of the effects on other people and on the environment. This might lead to a discussion about whether we need to adjust our lifestyles to take account of the downsides of globalisation, for instance be prepared not to have or do certain things in the interests of sustainability. This provides a context and framework for the spreads that follow on child labour and tourism.

3.3 Hard labour!

Pupil's Book pp. 70–75
Activity sheet 22

These three spreads focus on the issue of child labour and how active citizens in the UK could take action to improve the situation for the children involved. The **Activity** on page 70 introduces pupils to four case studies of children working in different industries and to the United Nations Convention on the Rights of the Child on page 72. It asks them to read the studies in the light of an extract from the Convention to appreciate how their work impacts their lives. The fourth case study on the chocolate industry is picked up on page 75 as a campaigning issue. A full version of the Convention adapted for young people can be found on **Activity sheet 22**.

Pages 72–74 The United Nations Convention on the Rights of the Child

The **Discuss** activity on page 73 adds a UK perspective to show how child protection laws operate in the UK. However, pupils may not agree with some of these laws: some young people would like the opportunity to work in order to earn extra money and others may feel that measures that stop them buying things like fireworks are unreasonable. You could hold a spot-debate on child protection laws, particularly related to work. This involves dividing the class in half, with one half arguing in favour of the laws and the other half against; some might have to argue for views they do not personally hold. Each person is only allowed to speak twice in the debate and can only speak when they are handed a 'speaking stick' (any object you choose). The debate is conducted in a sharp, fast way with little or no preparation.

On page 73, pupils are asked to consider what they as global consumers can do about child labour. Of course, some pupils may argue that it is nothing to do with them as there is nothing they can really do about it anyway and they should be able to take advantage of cheap goods. The statements are designed to stimulate discussion by bringing in a range of arguments and raise the issue of powerlessness in an international arena. The end result of most discussions tends to be that products involving the use of child labour should be banned. This seems to be a simple and effective solution. The next spread, however, is designed to challenge this view and make them aware of the complexities of the issue and the danger of coming up with easy solutions.

As the **Activity** on page 74 demonstrates, the working children themselves do not want outright bans or boycotts. In many countries children are a part of the local economy and help support and maintain their families. If the products they make were boycotted, then it is likely that the children and their families would suffer enormously. The alternatives to child labour may be worse, as the diagram on page 74 shows. Some children are likely to become involved in back-breaking agricultural work while, even worse, some may be forced into the child sex trade. So, while it is clear that some forms of child labour should be

This is Citizenship 1 Teacher's Resource Book

Section 3: Being a global citizen

stopped immediately, the children themselves want to be allowed to work as long as certain conditions are met, for example working for a limited number of hours so that they can have the opportunity to be educated and have some leisure time. It is important that pupils realise that issues like these are not always as cut and dried as they would appear.

Page 75 Taking action

The final part of this sequence of spreads looks at the sort of action the pupils, as global citizens, could take to bring about change. The case study of Gallions Primary School is used to show that even relatively young children can mount a campaign and have quite a considerable impact, reaching the national media and putting the chocolate industry on the defensive. The children benefited enormously from this: gaining in self-confidence and acquiring skills and knowledge about how to prosecute a campaign. It is a good example of active citizenship and experiential learning.

There is a lot of material on child labour on the internet. You might want to tap into the campaigns that are running when you are teaching this topic. The charity websites can be a way of making contact with the main campaigns. There are also schemes to protect children through quality marks such as Rugmark. These directly inform consumers that the product can be regarded as made without using exploited labour, particularly children.

What is clear is that the pressure exerted by campaigns and in the media does make companies change their practices and check the conditions of the workforce used to manufacture their products. Some companies have become involved in supporting educational and related activities in communities where workplaces are located. Companies do not like bad publicity in this area. So citizens in this country can play a role in improving things for people in developing countries where the products they consume are made.

3.4 What is fair trade?

Pupil's Book pp. 76–77
Activity sheets 23, 24, 25, 26, 27, 28, 29, 30, 31

Fair trade has not been given a huge amount of space in this textbook because most pupils have been introduced to the topic in primary school or in geography classes. Here we have concentrated on what fair trade means and what the Fairtrade Mark seeks to guarantee. However, if you want to pursue this topic further we have included in this Teacher's Resource Book a detailed explanation of fair trade and more classroom materials, including a game, that you might like to use with your pupils (see below).

This decision-making **Activity** on page 76 asks pupils to consider three products and decide which should be awarded the Fairtrade Mark. It will give pupils a greater understanding of what the Fairtrade Mark means, and help them to become better informed consumers. The chart on page 77 is reproduced in a slightly simpler form on **Activity sheet 23**. This can be handed out to groups of pupils. Each group could present their final decisions to the class. It is important for pupils to understand that some farmers work as individuals, on a small scale, whereas others are employed as workers on plantations and may experience different types of problems. Key terms, such as 'sustainable development', may also need to be reinforced here. The answers to the Activity are:

- Sugar would get the Mark.
- Tea would not get the Mark.
- Brazil nuts are up for discussion but would only be given the Mark in the future if they meet certain conditions, for example the pay and treatment of the families who collect the nuts need to be improved.

What is fair trade all about?

Many farmers in the developing world who grow products such as tea, coffee and cocoa

This is Citizenship 1 Teacher's Resource Book

Section 3: Being a global citizen

are poor and getting poorer. They do not have the resources to market their goods directly, so they only get a small share of the true market price – sometimes even below the cost of harvesting their crop. Because prices are so unpredictable they cannot plan their future, and they can only borrow money at excessive interest rates. Such debts are often a part of life, as farmers have nothing left to live on until they can sell their harvested crop. As a result, many small farmers:

- have poor and uncertain incomes
- are unable to look after their crop effectively
- cannot educate their children
- cannot maintain their homes properly.

Similarly, many plantation workers do not see the benefits of increasing world trade. Too often they:

- endure unsafe working conditions
- live in very poor and basic housing
- lack the opportunity to join a union, or participate in decisions that affect their lives on the plantation.

Fair trade is an alternative approach to international trade. It is about establishing and maintaining fair terms of trade with disadvantaged communities in the developing world, enabling them to achieve greater security and control over their own lives. The Fairtrade Foundation was set up by CAFOD (Catholic Fund for Overseas Development), Christian Aid, New Consumer, Oxfam, Traidcraft Exchange and the World Development Movement. The Foundation awards a consumer label, the Fairtrade Mark, to products that meet internationally recognised standards of fair trade. In the UK, the first Fairtrade Mark products appeared in 1994 (chocolate and coffee). Sales have expanded rapidly and they now include a wide variety of products. The Fairtrade Foundation, with its partners, checks that approved products continue to meet defined criteria.

Some key concepts for pupils to understand when investigating trade and fair trade are:

- The rules of international trade favour the rich countries of the North over the poorer countries of the South.
- The North depends on commodities from the South, and the South relies on being able to sell basic goods to the North – interdependence.
- Prices for these goods can fluctuate widely. The supply chain from producer to consumer is often a complex one, with products changing hands many times before they reach the shops.
- Working conditions for producers are often poor, with low wages, a lack of safety standards and no job security. Environmental degradation is often a consequence of production.
- Fair trade offers an active way to overcome these injustices and promote more sustainable development. The Fairtrade Mark guarantees a better deal for producers in the South.
- Actions by individuals in one part of the world can have an impact on individuals in other parts of the world.

The injustices of world trade can be illustrated using the envelope simulation described below. 'The Trading Game' and 'The Chocolate Game', both available through Oxfam, are also useful resources for demonstrating interdependence.

The following activity can be used to help pupils develop a sense of empathy with producers and illustrates the difficulties they face. It can be run in 15 minutes or longer, as required. Give pupils some scrap paper to make envelopes. Glue or tape and scissors will be needed. Stress that this needs to be a 'quality' product. Impose strict quality control checks – size, straight lines, neat edges. As they complete their envelopes, ask pupils to come up with a price for what they are producing. Listen to their suggestions, encourage them to reach some agreement, and then respond by making them an offer for the envelopes that is only a tiny fraction of their named price. Refuse to negotiate – tell them you are the only buyer for miles around, and

This is Citizenship 1 Teacher's Resource Book

Section 3: Being a global citizen

that if they don't accept your offer you'll buy your envelopes from another class. After the activity, ask pupils:

- how long it took to make one envelope
- how many they could make in a day
- how much they thought they needed to earn
- how they felt about the price you offered them
- what choices they had and whether there were any alternatives.

Discuss parallels with the 'real' world, for example:

- the problems of maintaining quality
- what happens when buyers reject products that don't conform to standards set
- having to accept a very low price – producers are often so desperate for money by the time a crop ripens that they will sell at a very low price.

More materials on fair trade

Activity sheet 24 contains the case study of the Peck family to provide information on the way fair trade has changed the life of one small producer and demonstrates the sorts of difficulties the Pecks faced before they entered a fair trade agreement.

Activity sheet 25, 'The UK and world trade', provides some statements to provoke thought about the way the UK trades with other countries. Photocopy and cut up the statements and use the 'diamond nine' method to rank the statements. This method forces pupils to choose the statements they consider most important without having to put them in a linear rank order. It encourages them to discuss the order in their pairs or groups. Pupils could then be asked to explain, and justify, the statements with which they most strongly agree/disagree. This can lead on to discussion work, drawing out the advantages and disadvantages of world trade and fair trade.

Once pupils have been introduced to the Fairtrade Mark and fair trade criteria, they can play the Trade Trap game. This is on **Activity sheets 26–31**. The game is designed to deepen pupils' understanding of how world trade operates and to help pupils empathise with producers. They can then take control of the game themselves, adapting and developing it to reflect different circumstances. It helps them to think about and express their own views about trade and promotes their interest in fair trade.

Pupils play the game in groups of three or four. Each has to survive as a poor producer, with a range of difficulties to contend with. They may well become caught up in a cycle of poverty and debt, from which they have no opportunity to escape. Some will be able to enter the fair trade market (by way of the chance cards) and experience some of the differences this can make. If few pupils get onto the fair trade track, you might have to throw in your own chance cards. At the end of the game you need to be able to compare the experiences of those who were able to go on the fair trade track with those who were not.

The rules of the game can be found on **Activity sheet 26** and the game board on **Activity sheet 27**. You will need to photocopy both and, if possible, enlarge the game board so that it fits on A3 paper. Pupils record what happens to them in the game on the money chart, which can be found on **Activity sheet 28**. The trade cards and chance cards can be photocopied from **Activity sheets 29, 30** and **31**. The easiest way to play the game is to duplicate sets of cards, which the pupils can place face down on the game board. They pick up a card when they land on the appropriate square. An alternative way to play is for pupils to throw two dice to see what card they get. The dice numbers are in brackets on the card.

After an initial round, or an agreed number of 'years', pupils can develop the game themselves, for example by adding more chance cards, and completing the 'blank' squares on the game board. They may also try changing/adapting the rules. Alternatively, depending on the ability range of the group, the game could be

Section 3: Being a global citizen

made more challenging by introducing it as incomplete – all 'trade' and 'chance' cards could then be generated by the pupils themselves.

Criteria for winning the game should also be discussed. Are the winners those who are in the most secure financial position after an agreed number of years? Or are they those who have managed to improve their quality of life the most?

The following questions could form the basis for debriefing after playing the game.

- What happened? What were your main problems/successes according to the money chart?
- What did you feel about things as the game went on?
- How did things change for those who were able to sell their produce to a fair trade company?
- Was it always 'good news' for the fair trade farmers, and 'bad news' for the rest?
- What was realistic about the game?
- How did your changes to the game make it more/less realistic?
- How can we have an effect on the real world situation in which most poor farmers find themselves?

3.5 How can charities help?

Pupil's Book pp. 78–81
Activity sheets 32, 33

This subsection could act as a way of introducing the topic of charities and their role in the world as well as helping to prepare pupils to take part in work with charities and to mount their own charitable campaign. The aim of the first spread is to introduce pupils to the work of voluntary organisations in the international arena. Pupils will know about the work of charities, particularly in relation to disasters and their impacts, for example hunger, disease, homelessness, but they may not be so aware of their longer-term development work. The **Activity** on page 78 informs pupils about the different ways that charities provide aid. In the **Discuss** questions on page 79, pupils focus on the concrete application of these methods with examples from Oxfam and WaterAid. There is, of course, a huge amount of information on the internet about the international work of charities. Pupils could research the work of different charities and report their findings back to the rest of the class (see 'Websites' in the Resources section). It would be very useful to have a speaker from an international charity to visit the class and talk about the work of the charity. Addresses and contact numbers of some of the main international charities can be found on the relevant websites listed in the Resources section.

Page 80 Should you help?

Support for charities is not entirely straightforward. Some people feel worn out by the almost incessant demand for charities for more and more funds – so-called 'compassion fatigue'. Others question the way charities collect donations using, in some cases, high-pressure sales techniques to get people to sign up for direct debits. Other arguments focus on the way the money is spent and how much goes on the administration of the charity; also on whether the money genuinely brings long-lasting results that are of benefit to the recipients.

If pupils are going to be asked to participate in fundraising then it is an important matter to debate. The **Discuss** activity on page 80 asks pupils to examine the arguments and to discuss them. **Activity sheet 32** provides the arguments on a grid which pupils can mark as 'agree', 'disagree' or 'can't decide'. Pupils can add other arguments in the blank rows. This could then lead on to a full-scale discussion of the issue.

Page 81 Developing your campaigning skills

Campaigning is an important aspect of active citizenship. The **Activity** on page 81 is designed to help pupils become aware of what's involved in running a campaign but

This is Citizenship 1 Teacher's Resource Book

Section 3: Being a global citizen

also to help them to start to develop some of the skills involved. In this Activity they are only asked to draw up a plan of what they would do, but there is no reason why they should not choose an issue and conduct a campaign. They might raise awareness of the issue in the school by designing posters and leaflets but also pass on their concerns by writing letters to local councillors or MPs. Alternatively they could join in a campaign already being run by a charity. It is part of their citizenship education that they realise how campaigns are conducted, involving:

- a clear issue and specific aims for the campaign
- researching the issue thoroughly so that they can raise awareness amongst others
- working out who to target so the campaign is effective
- deciding on the best methods to reach the target audience
- carrying these out effectively, whether it is giving presentations, writing leaflets or running fundraising events.

It would be very helpful to involve charity workers who have experience of running campaigns. They could support the pupils, help them develop their skills and provide information about what they do in practice.

Many schools provide pupils with the opportunity to raise funds for various charities. **Activity sheet 33** gives some ideas for fundraising events and also provides space for pupils to write in their own final ideas. Give copies of this sheet to pairs or groups of pupils. Organisations such as Comic Relief produce packs to help you to run a fundraising event.

3.6 How does tourism affect people?

Pupil's Book pp. 82–87
Activity sheets 34, 35, 36, 37

Tourism is the fastest-growing industry in the world and is set to expand enormously in the future. Millions of jobs in countries around the world depend on the tourist trade. However, there is increasing concern about the impact of tourism on some countries, particularly those which have natural environments and traditional cultures that are not centred on a money economy, materialism and consumerism.

The **Activity** on page 82 introduces pupils to the sorts of things many tourists today expect and demand from the places they visit. There is a good deal of scope here to bring in pupils' own holiday experiences. They could be asked about the sorts of things their families look for in resorts and what they require to make their holiday enjoyable. They could be encouraged to talk about the sorts of places they have visited or where they have lived and to discuss what is offered to attract tourists.

Some pupils will not have been on foreign holidays but there is a good chance that they are affected in some way by tourism, particularly if they live near areas of natural beauty, airports, or cities and towns visited by tourists. Tourism affects us as well as people in other countries, albeit that we are focusing on the international perspective here. So the task on page 83 is designed as a little aside to bring in the pupils' experience of how tourism affects them. This will of course make them more aware of how tourism affects people in other countries.

Pages 84–85 The benefits and costs of tourism

The **Activity** on page 85 considers the benefits and problems associated with tourism and begins to open up the issue of its impact on the local people and environment. The statements are used to help pupils think about the issue and to engage them in discussion. They can be found on **Activity sheet 34** so that you can reproduce them should you want pupils to physically sort them into categories. This can be very helpful to pupils with literacy problems. Again, pupils could be asked to offer their own observations about the positive and negative impacts of tourism on the places they have visited. Pupils are likely

48 *This is Citizenship 1 Teacher's Resource Book*

Section 3: Being a global citizen

to come to the conclusion that tourism can be beneficial but that unfettered tourism can be destructive if it is not controlled or managed. This leads on nicely to the next activity.

Pages 86–87 How would you develop tourism in Myssia?

Myssia is a composite fabrication designed to represent some of the issues raised by the growth of tourism in different parts of the world. The aim of the **Activity** on page 87 is to open up the debate over the advantages and disadvantages of developing tourism in a natural environment where there is a stable culture and strong religious heritage. In the initial part of the Activity the pupils are encouraged to think as tour operators who wish to develop Myssia as a holiday resort. They might decide to put in some of the attractions from pages 82–83: hotels, swimming pools, bars and nightclubs.

Then they are asked to consider the likely impacts on different groups in Myssia. Some of these groups would benefit in some ways. It would offer opportunities for employment and probably improvements in the standard of living, particularly for young people and families, and for fishermen and farmers who would find markets for their products. However, elders, religious leaders and others might not like the changes this brings about in term of the ways the tourists behave, their dress and possibly poor behaviour (for example, drunkenness). Also, real examples have shown that fishermen sometimes lose their harbours to marinas and tourist activities (for example, jetskiing) and do not get rewarded adequately. Similarly farmers might lose land for development and find themselves short of water, which goes to the hotels and restaurants. So it's not straightforward.

In the last part of the Activity, pupils are asked to reach some balanced judgements about the development referring to the tenets of responsible tourism. These have been drawn from websites set up to promote responsible tourism which can be found on the internet. There are a number of schemes designed to encourage ethical or green tourism and a significant number of tour operators have signed up to codes of practice designed to protect the environment and support the local economy.

The issue of economic development is an important one. Many people in developing countries want material goods and a higher standard of living, so it is not simply a choice of development or no development. Many want development but in a way that protects their environment and their culture and does not pull apart their traditional way of life. Of course, there are others, including many developers, who just want the rewards regardless of the cost.

A more engaging and stimulating way to bring these issues to life for pupils is to run the role play that is included on **Activity sheets 35–37**. This role play will occupy several sessions. Alternatively, it could be run in a longer session in which other curriculum subjects participate, since it involves understanding, skills and abilities from a range of subjects, for example English, geography and RE. By asking pupils to take on the roles of different groups, the pupils will more readily be able to think about how the development might affect the different groups.

The briefing sheet for the role play can be found on **Activity sheet 35**. This sets out the context of the simulation, the groups involved and the instructions for running it. You could give two or three copies to each group. This is a 'meeting' simulation where different groups discuss their ideas. There are eight groups in all and you should decide how you are going to allocate pupils to them (see below). It would be helpful if pupils could have their roles to look at before the main session. If you do not have enough pupils to fill all the groups, you can combine some; you could put elders and religious leaders together in one group and similarly the unemployed with parents of young children and teenagers.

The allocation of roles is important. The role cards on **Activity sheet 36** can be reproduced and handed out to pupils. The

This is Citizenship 1 Teacher's Resource Book

Section 3: Being a global citizen

roles of the tour operators and government are crucial and the pupils playing these roles will probably need more time to prepare. The tour operators need time to draw up proposals for their development and maybe produce some illustrations to go with their presentation. Holiday brochures could provide them with ideas for a resort complex. They could also draw a map of Myssia showing the positions of the proposed airport and holiday complexes and how wildlife safaris might work, for example with special lodges in the mountains for trips.

For this reason, the tour operators' group should be made up of pupils who are good at presentation and are able to respond on the hoof to questions and points raised by the other groups. The tour operators and government are going to have to be most responsive at the meeting, since local people are likely to put demands on them to give guarantees. Tell both parties that they can lie if they want to, promising things that they have no intention of doing. For instance, the tour operators can promise jobs and training but they know already that to get their hotels, etc. up and running they are going to have to bring in experienced staff.

The prompt sheet on **Activity sheet 37** will help groups who are finding it difficult to establish their position. You can use this to suggest points they might include or you can simply give them their prompt at a key point to help them along.

After the pupils have taken the vote, go round each group and ask them to explain:

- why they adopted the position they did
- what difficulties they had in reaching an agreement
- whether they would change it in the light of the meeting.

Use their responses to pull out the main issues about development versus the possible negative effects on their existing way of life:

- Ask the tour operators and the government whether they deliberately lied.
- Ask the groups if any of them feel dissatisfied and let down by the final decision in the vote.
- Ask the groups as a whole what conditions they would put on any development of tourism in Myssia.
- Ask them whether they feel this simulation might reflect what happens in real life.

Reflection

As in Sections 1 and 2, we have provided some suggestions for ways in which pupils can assess their own learning and progress. Pupils can rate their own skills levels using the chart, but should try to provide evidence to back up their score and suggestions for improvement. The understanding is checked through sentence completion, short answers and peer review. See the notes in this Teacher's Resource Book for Section 1 (pages 8–9).

Activity sheet 21

What do you know about other countries?

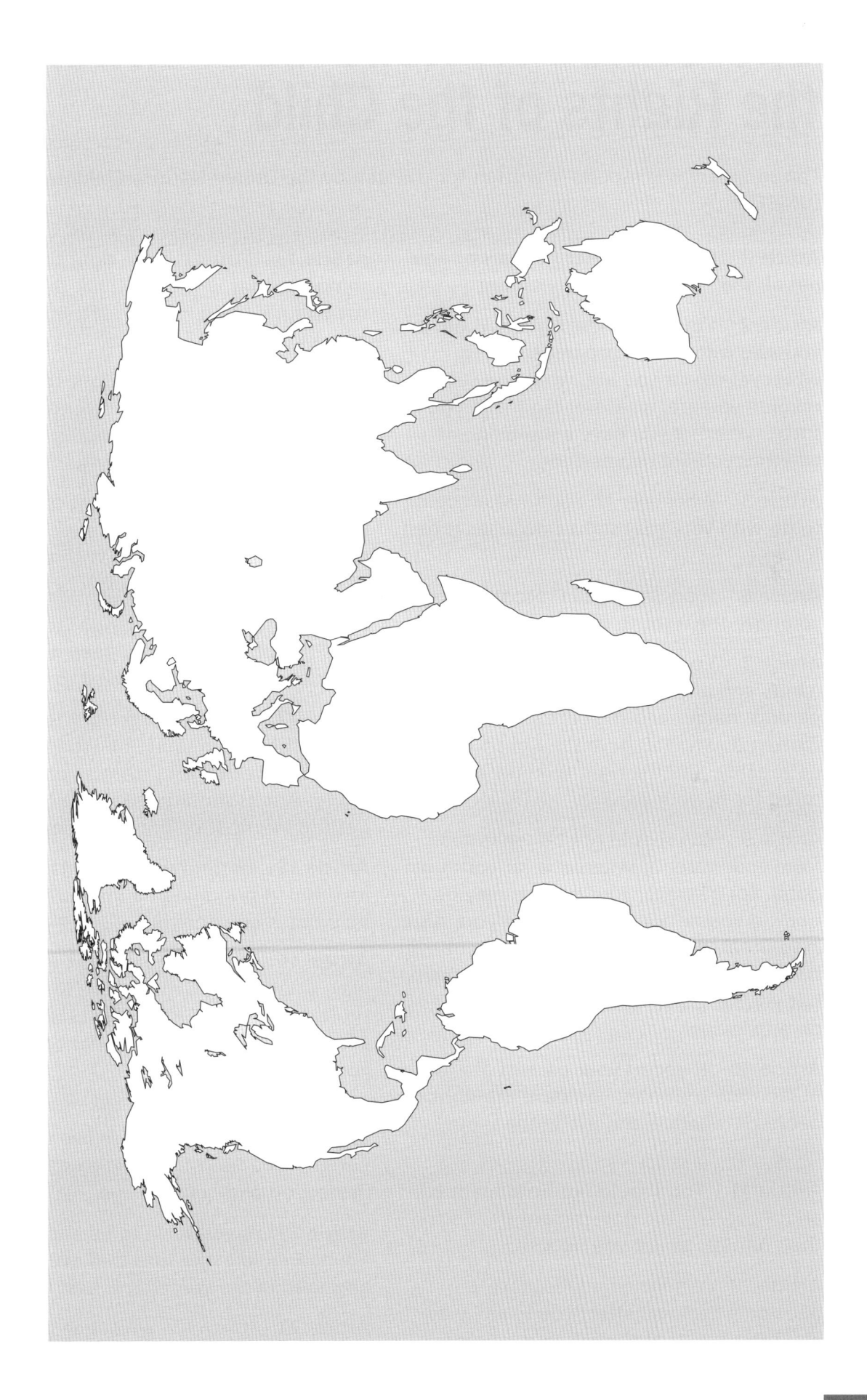

© Hodder Education, 2008 *This is Citizenship 1 Teacher's Resource Book*

Activity sheet 22

The United Nations Convention on the Rights of the Child

This summary was especially written for children by the United Nations Children's Fund (UNICEF).

Article 1 Everyone under 18 years of age has all the rights in this Convention.

Article 2 You have these rights, whoever you are, whoever your parents are, whatever colour you are, whatever sex or religion you are, whatever language you speak, whether you have a disability, or whether you are rich or poor.

Article 3 Whenever an adult has anything to do with you, they should do what is best for you.

Article 6 Everyone should recognise that you have the right to live.

Article 7 You have the right to have a name, and at your birth, your name, your parents' names and the date should be written down. You have the right to a nationality, and the right to know and be cared for by your parents.

Article 9 You should not be separated from your parents, unless it is for your own good. For instance, your parents may be hurting you or not taking care of you. Also, if your parents decide to live apart, you will have to live with one or the other of them, but you have the right to contact both parents easily.

Article 10 If you or your parents are living in separate countries, you have the right to get back together and live in the same place.

Article 11 You should not be kidnapped, and if you are, the government should try their hardest to get you back.

Article 12 Whenever adults make a decision which will affect you in any way, you have the right to give your opinion, and the adults have to take that seriously.

Article 13 You have the right to find out things and say what you think through speaking, writing, making art, etc., unless it attacks the rights of others.

Article 14 You have the right to think what you like and be whatever religion you want to be. Your parents should help you learn what is right and wrong.

Article 15 You have the right to meet, make friends and make clubs with other people, unless it interferes with the rights of others.

Article 16 You have the right to a private life. For instance, you can keep a diary that other people are not allowed to see.

Article 17 You have the right to collect information from radio, newspapers, television, books, etc., from all around the world. Adults should make sure that you get the information you can understand.

Article 18 Both of your parents should be involved in bringing you up and they should do what is best for you.

Article 19 No one should hurt you in any way. Adults should make sure that you are protected from abuse, violence and neglect. Even your parents have no right to hurt you.

Article 20 If you do not have any parents, or if it is not safe for you to live with your parents, you have the right to special protection and help.

Article 21 If you have to be adopted, adults should make sure that everything is arranged in the way that is best for you.

Article 22 If you are a refugee (meaning you have to leave your own country because it is not safe for you to live there),

This is Citizenship 1 Teacher's Resource Book © Hodder Education, 2008

you have the right to special protection and help.

Article 23 If you are disabled, either mentally or physically, you have the right to special care and education to help you grow up in the same way as other children.

Article 24 You have a right to good health. This means that you should have professional care and medicines when you are sick. Adults should try their hardest to make sure that children do not get sick in the first place by feeding and taking good care of them.

Article 27 You have the right to a good enough 'standard of living'. This means that parents have the responsibility to make sure you have food, clothes, a place to live, etc. If parents cannot afford this, the government should help.

Article 28 You have a right to education. You must have primary education, and it must be free. You should also be able to go to secondary school.

Article 29 The purpose of your education is to develop your personality, talents and mental and physical abilities to the fullest. Education should also develop your respect for your parents, your cultural identity and for the cultural background and values of others, and prepare you to live responsibly and peacefully, in a free society, understanding the rights of other people, and respecting the environment.

Article 30 If you come from a minority group, you have the right to enjoy your own culture, practise your own religion and use your own language.

Article 31 You have a right to play and leisure.

Article 32 You have the right to be protected from working places or conditions that are likely to damage your health or get in the way of your education. If somebody is making money out of your work, you should be paid fairly.

Article 33 You have the right to be protected from illegal drugs and from the business of making and selling drugs.

Article 34 You have the right to be protected from sexual abuse. This means that nobody can do anything to your body that you do not want them to do, such as touching you or taking pictures of you or making you say things that you don't want to say.

Article 35 No one is allowed to kidnap or sell you.

Article 37 Even if you do something wrong, no one is allowed to punish you in a way that humiliates you or hurts you badly. You should never be put in prison except as a last resort, and, if you are put in prison, you have the right to special care and regular visits from your family.

Article 38 You have a right to protection in times of war. If you are under fifteen, you should not have to be in an army or take part in a battle.

Article 39 If you have been hurt or neglected in any way, for instance in a war, you have the right to special care and treatment.

Article 40 You have the right to defend yourself if you have been accused of committing a crime. The police and the lawyers and the judges in court should treat you with respect and make sure you understand everything that is going on.

Article 42 All adults and all children should know about this Convention. You have a right to learn about your rights and adults should learn about them too.

Activity sheet 23

Do they meet the Fairtrade Mark?

Use this table with the Activity on page 76.

Fairtrade Mark criteria	Tea	Brazil nuts	Sugar
• Price covers production costs			
• Decent wages			
• Decent housing			
• Health and safety standards enforced			
• No child or forced labour			
• Some money reinvested to improve conditions			
• Environment treated with care			
• Union membership allowed			
• Long-term plans for improvement			
• Advance payments			
Total score for each product			

Recommendation

Activity sheet 24

Fair trade case study: the Peck family

Chocolate is made from cocoa beans, which only grow where there is a hot climate. Two-thirds of the world's cocoa is grown by 'smallholders' – individual farmers who work for themselves. The Peck family tell their story:

'I'm Christina Peck. We live in a small, simple cabin in Belize, Central America. Our home is basic – we have no electricity, or indoor water supply. We are cocoa farmers. It's hard work. The crops have to be carefully tended; then, once the cocoa pods have been picked, the beans have to be dried. Justino has to carry a 45 kg sack of beans on his back, across two miles of rough roads. Then he has a two-hour bus journey to the warehouse, where the beans are stored before being shipped to Europe, where they're made into chocolate for you to eat.'

'I'm Justino. About ten years ago we were managing on the money we earned from selling cocoa beans. We could buy the basic things we needed. Then, suddenly, the price of cocoa fell, and our beans were only worth half what they had been. We had no money to buy food and clothes – things were desperate for us and our neighbours. We got together and set up a co-operative. This meant we could work together to transport and market our cocoa, keeping our costs down. But we had to borrow money to do this and it became more and more difficult to repay our debts. Some of our neighbours had no choice but to give up, leave their land and look for work on plantations or in the city.

'Then, out of the blue, we were approached by Green & Black's, the UK chocolate company, who wanted to buy our cocoa! They offered us a much higher price for our beans and guaranteed to pay it for three years, buying all the cocoa we could produce. They used our cocoa to make 'Maya Gold' chocolate, the first brand to be given the Fairtrade Mark. Now life is much better. Farmers have returned to their villages to grow cocoa. Communities are back together again.

'We've used some of the money to make a concrete floor in our house – before, we just had a dirt floor. We can now afford to send our children to secondary school, as well as buying them school books and shoes. We've planted more cocoa, because of our confidence in fair trade – it really does make a difference.'

© Hodder Education, 2008 *This is Citizenship 1 Teacher's Resource Book*

Activity sheet 25

The UK and world trade

Read the statements on the cards below. Cut them up and arrange them in the shape of a diamond, as in the diagram, to show how strongly you agree, or disagree, with them. Put the statement you agree with most strongly at the top, the two next strongest statements on the second row and so on. Put the one you agree with least at the bottom. When you have finished, have a class discussion to see if everybody agrees on these issues.

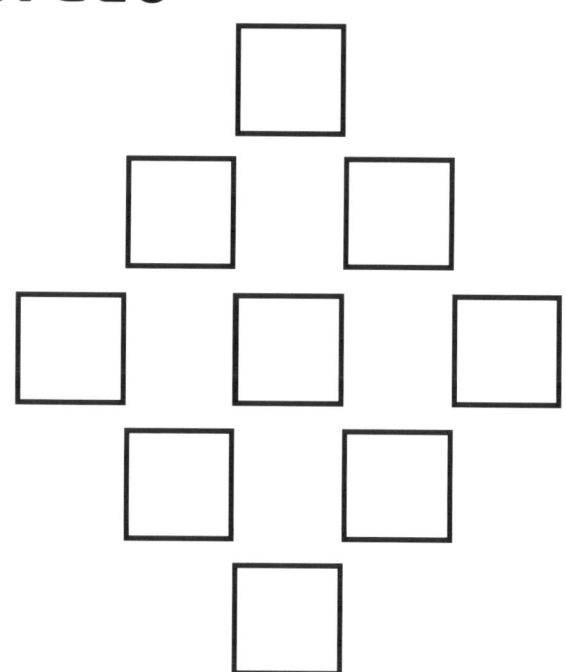

A If farmers in the developing world had fewer children, and worked harder, they'd be better off.	**B** If we buy fair trade products, we can make a difference to the lives of thousands of farmers in the developing world.	**C** Farmers in the UK deserve more support than farmers on the other side of the world.
D Supermarkets in the UK should provide the consumer with food at the lowest possible prices.	**E** Multinational companies which control much of the world's trade are a good thing – they provide jobs for thousands of people in rich and poor countries.	**F** The main thing to change is us – we should be prepared to pay a little more for fair trade products.
G The UK should import less food from countries where people don't have enough to eat.	**H** Fair trade foods taste just as good, or better, than other brands.	**I** It's up to the governments of developing countries to help their poor, not up to UK consumers.

Activity sheet 26

Trade Trap – a fair trade game

You are a poor farmer in a developing country. Each year you sell your crop to traders, who sell it on to a big multinational company. Play the game and find out what life is like for you and your family.

If you're lucky, you could be selling in the fair trade market, and you'll see what difference this makes to your quality of life.

How to play

- Play in groups of four to six. Everyone will need a counter. You will need a dice (or two, if you are going to use the game cards).
- Before you start, everyone needs to draw up a *money chart* (see page 59). You already have $100 from selling your last crop. Use the *Cost of living* tables to help you decide how to spend it.
- Put your counters on **START**, and throw the dice in turn. Whoever has the lowest score moves forward first, following the outer 'world trade' track.
- Take turns, making sure that any instructions on the squares are followed carefully. If you land on **WORLD TRADE** or **FAIR TRADE CHANCE**, pick up a chance card from the correct pile.
- Every round of the board represents one year. As you pass **TRADE**, pick up a trade card to find out how much money you get for that year's crop.
- Decide how to spend your money each year. You may have debts to pay and some difficult decisions to make. Keep a full record on your *money chart*.
- At the end of the game, see who is in the best situation – consider money and quality of life.

When you've played for several 'years', think about ways of developing the game. You could:

- alter the rules
- adapt the costs
- add more chance cards
- fill in other squares on the board
- change some of the trade cards.

Cost of living

These costs are for your whole family, for one year.

Essential items

These *must* be paid for each year, because it's hard to survive without them. If you can't afford them, you'll have to borrow money.

Basic housing	$10
Basic food	$50
Basic clothes	$30

Desirable items

You'll have to decide what you can afford each year – try to provide all these things for your family if you possibly can:

School	$30
School books	$10
Shoes	$10
More food or clothes	$25
Home improvements	$15

© Hodder Education, 2008 *This is Citizenship 1 Teacher's Resource Book*

Activity sheet 27

Trade Trap game board

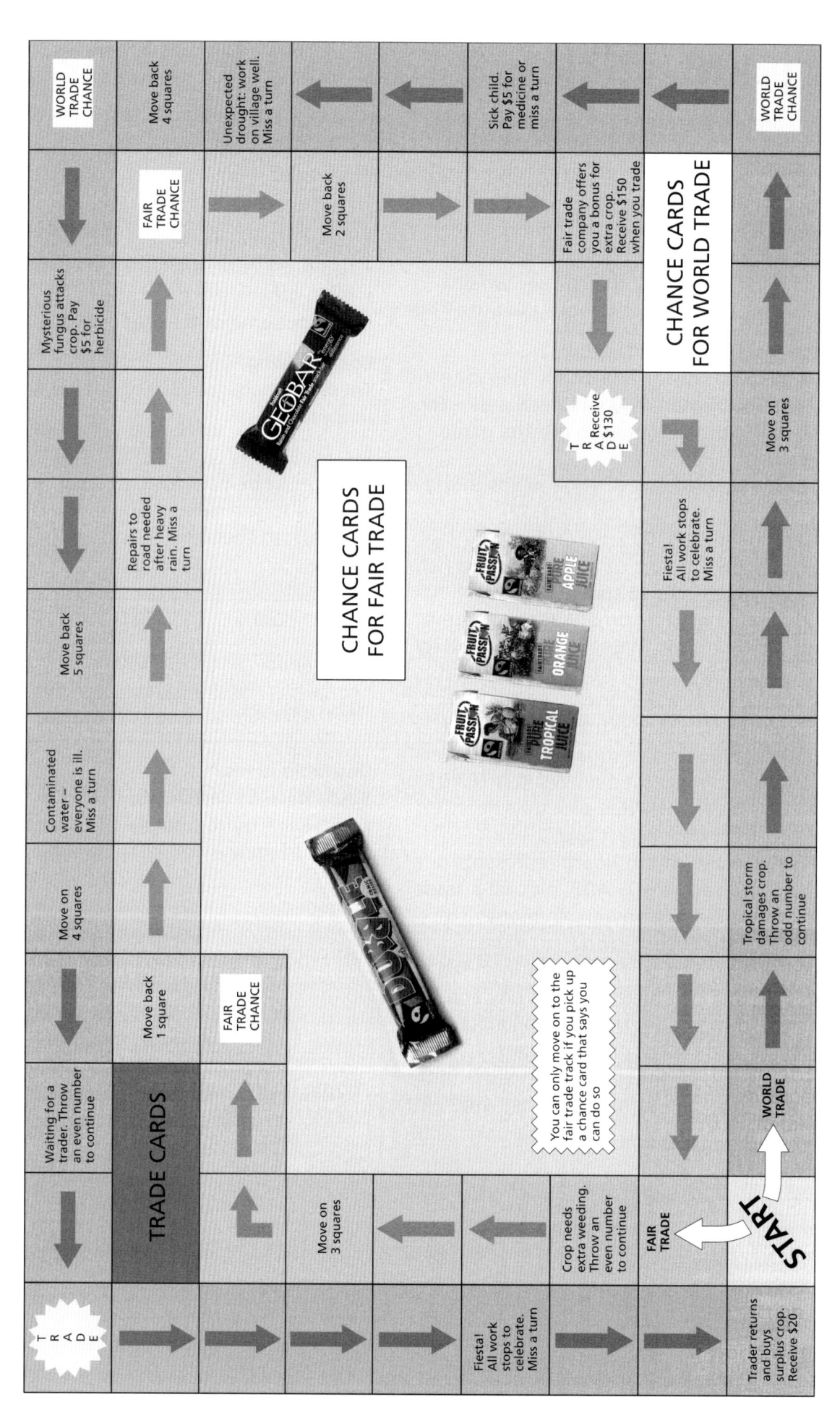

Activity sheet 28

Money chart

Year	Money received	Items bought (cost)	Total spent	Money owed	Balance	Comment
1	$100					
2						
3						
4						
5						
6						
7						
8						
9						
10						

© Hodder Education, 2008 *This is Citizenship 1 Teacher's Resource Book*

Activity sheet 29

Trade cards

Use this sheet with the Trade Trap game. Cut up the cards and place them in a pile face down on the game board. Pick one up as you pass **TRADE**.

World price rise! Your crop is worth 20 per cent more than you were expecting – receive $120. (2)

Your usual trader doesn't come to your village this year. A new 'middleman' appears. You are desperate for money to live on, so have to accept the $70 he offers you. (8)

Trader cash crisis! Your trader has no cash to pay you. Instead he gives you basic food and clothes – receive no cash. (3)

A month ago, pests attacked your crop. Half of it was ruined. The trader will only give you $60. (9)

Your trader's scales are 'fixed'. Your crop weighs 10 per cent less than you expected it to – receive only $90. (4)

The trader says he is not impressed by the quality of your crop this year. He says it's below standard. He offers you $90 – take it or leave it! (10)

The world price for your crop has fallen. It's only worth half what you had expected – receive $50. (5)

Receive $100. (11)

Serious crop failure in another part of the world means there's a shortage of the crop you grow. It's worth more this year! Receive $110. (6)

If you throw 12, throw again. (12)

A bumper harvest means there's a 'glut' of your crop on the world market. Your trader only offers you $80 – take it or leave it! (7)

This is Citizenship 1 Teacher's Resource Book © Hodder Education, 2008

World trade chance cards

Cut up the cards and place them in a pile face down on the game board. Pick up a card when you land on **WORLD TRADE CHANCE** on the 'world trade' track.

Your roof is leaking badly. Miss a turn to fix it. (2 or 3)	Your mother is ill. Walk with her to the hospital (a two-day round trip – miss a go), or pay $2 for a taxi. (10)
Your son needs to start secondary school. It will cost you $50 all together – he must have books and shoes for the long walk. You can borrow the money, but will have to pay back $55 when you next trade. (4 or 5)	Rats have got into your food store. You need to buy more basic food – cost $10. (If you borrow the money, pay back $11 next time you trade.) (11)
The government has introduced a new land tax. Pay $5 now. (If you have to borrow the money, pay back $6 when you next trade.) (6)	Your neighbours suggest you join their new co-operative. You must pay $5 now, but the tools you can share mean your crop will be better – you will earn an extra $15 when you next trade. (12)
Fantastic news! A fair trade company says it will buy the entire crop you and your neighbours produce (as long as you agree to certain conditions). You can move on to the 'fair trade' track next time you reach start. (7, 8 or 9)	

© Hodder Education, 2008 *This is Citizenship 1 Teacher's Resource Book*

Activity sheet 31

Fair trade chance cards

Cut up the cards and place them in a pile face down on the game board. Pick up a card when you land on **FAIR TRADE CHANCE** on the 'fair trade' track.

A new fair trade agreement means you will earn an extra $30 when you next trade. (2)	You are no longer able to meet the fair trade conditions for growing your crop. Return to start and the 'world trade' track now. (7 or 8)
You can no longer use weedkillers on your crop – miss a turn to do weeding. (3 or 4)	You offer to help build a new medical centre – throw 2, 4 or 6 to continue. (9)
Your children are all ill. Pay $10 for medical care. You can borrow this until you next trade if you need to. (5)	Your co-operative can now afford to build its own school. It will only cost you $20 to send your children there. (10)
Thanks to fair trade, you now have a regular water supply to the village. This means less time collecting water and more time to tend your crop – you produce more. Receive an extra $20 when you next trade. (6)	If you throw 11 or 12, throw again. (11 or 12)

This is Citizenship 1 Teacher's Resource Book © Hodder Education, 2008

Activity sheet 32

Should you help?

Look at each statement and think about whether you agree, disagree or can't decide. Put a tick in the relevant box. Add other arguments in the blank rows.

	Agree	Disagree	Can't decide
A We should always help people worse off than ourselves. It is morally the right thing to do.			
B If we don't help people in trouble, others might not help us when we are in need.			
C Other people's problems are nothing to do with me.			
D How can anyone see pictures of human suffering and not help? Especially when it's children.			
E Helping people in poor countries makes them dependent on aid. We should encourage them to help themselves.			
F We're just pouring money down a huge drain. We spend millions and there is not much to show for it.			
G The real problem is over-population. People in poor countries should have smaller families.			
H Poor countries are poor because of the way rich people treated them in the past. We owe it to poor countries to help them.			
I Money that I give to charity might end up in the pocket of someone dishonest, not helping people in need.			
J We should help people in this country before giving money for other countries.			
K It's a religious duty to help people wherever they live.			

© Hodder Education, 2008 *This is Citizenship 1 Teacher's Resource Book*

Activity sheet 33

Ideas for fundraising events

Which of the ideas below do you think you could use for fundraising? Do you have other ideas of your own? Put your final ideas in the box at the bottom of the sheet.

Cake sale	Running a book sale (donations from the class)
Taking and selling photographs	Making and selling posters, badges, calendars, greetings cards, friendship bracelets, etc.
Fashion show	Raffle
Various sponsored activities (silence, swim, walk, etc.)	Running a tuck shop or stationery shop
Showing DVDs at lunchtime	Writing and selling a magazine or newspaper
Talent show	Writing and selling guides to the local area
Putting on entertainment (music, play, review)	Cleaning cars

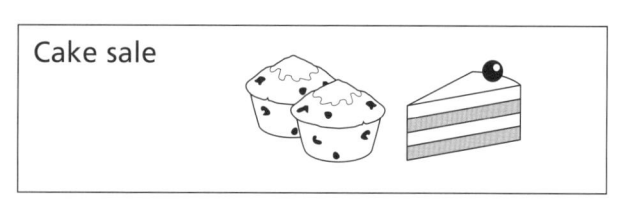

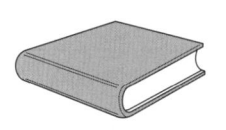

Our ideas for fundraising are:

1 _____

2 _____

This is Citizenship 1 Teacher's Resource Book © Hodder Education, 2008

Activity sheet 34

The benefits and problems of tourism

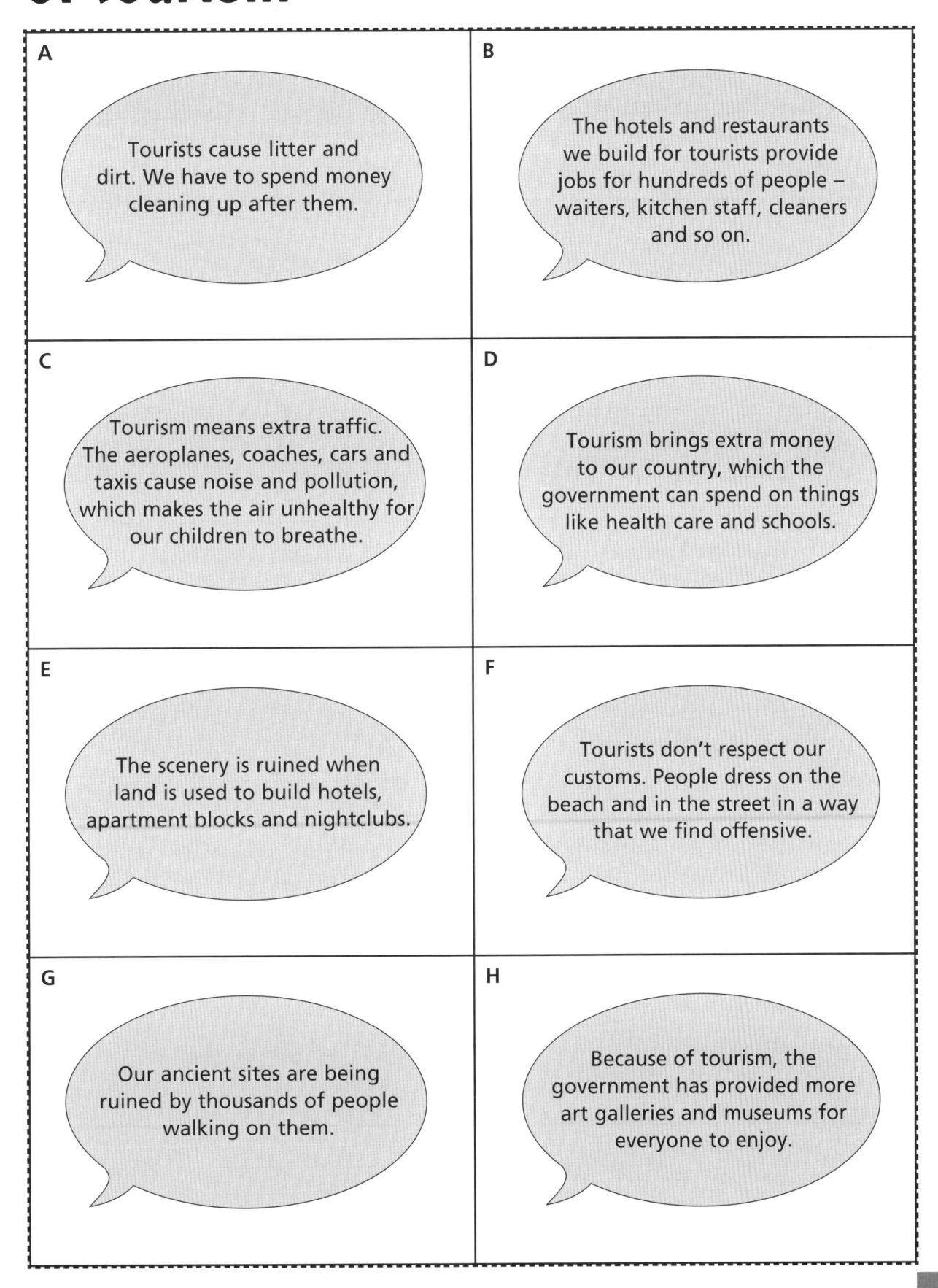

A Tourists cause litter and dirt. We have to spend money cleaning up after them.

B The hotels and restaurants we build for tourists provide jobs for hundreds of people – waiters, kitchen staff, cleaners and so on.

C Tourism means extra traffic. The aeroplanes, coaches, cars and taxis cause noise and pollution, which makes the air unhealthy for our children to breathe.

D Tourism brings extra money to our country, which the government can spend on things like health care and schools.

E The scenery is ruined when land is used to build hotels, apartment blocks and nightclubs.

F Tourists don't respect our customs. People dress on the beach and in the street in a way that we find offensive.

G Our ancient sites are being ruined by thousands of people walking on them.

H Because of tourism, the government has provided more art galleries and museums for everyone to enjoy.

© Hodder Education, 2008 *This is Citizenship 1 Teacher's Resource Book*

Activity sheet 34 (continued)

I Local people who want jobs in the tourist industry are willing to learn foreign languages and new skills.

J Young people get dissatisfied with their lives when they see how much money the foreign tourists have.

K We have terrible water shortages because of the swimming pools built for tourists.

L Tourists cause trouble in the bars and nightclubs.

M We have a beautiful country and we are proud that people want to visit us and find out more about us.

N Everyone is better off through tourism because all businesses get extra customers – ice-cream sellers, taxi drivers, market-stall holders – everyone.

O Local people cannot enjoy the tourist facilities because they are too expensive.

P Many local people can now buy all sorts of things they could not afford before the tourists came.

Developing Myssia – role-play simulation

Briefing

The potential for developing tourism in Myssia is enormous. There is space for buildings along the coast, and for an airport on the plains that could handle large jets. A number of foreign developers and tour operators wish to invest in the country. They want to build a large hotel complex and an airport. But before any plans can go ahead, they need permission from the government of Myssia. It is a democratic government that wants to put it to the people. Since Myssia has a small population, it is practical to consult everyone. The government has arranged a meeting of some of the main groups that are interested.

> Work in groups of four or five. Each group should take on a different role. The roles are:
> - foreign tour operators
> - government of Myssia
> - religious leaders
> - unemployed people
> - local farmers, fishermen and pearl divers
> - elders (much respected in Myssia)
> - parents of young children and teenagers
> - international environmentalists, for example Greenpeace.

Before the meeting

Read your role brief and, in your group, develop your arguments either for or against building an airport and a large hotel complex. Other developments, such as restaurants and shops, are likely to follow shortly afterwards if these two main ones go ahead.

- Think about how tourism would affect your group. Add any other points you can think of to the role brief.
- Talk about your group's position on tourism for Myssia and decide what arguments you will use in the meeting.
- Think about questions or demands you want to put to the foreign tour operators or to the government.
- Elect a spokesperson to put forward your point of view, although everyone will be able to speak at the meeting.

At the meeting

The government and the tour operators will sit at the front facing the audience. All other groups will sit in the audience. One member of the government (the Minister for Home Affairs) will chair the meeting. The tour operators should present their case first in no more than five minutes. Then people in the audience can make points and ask questions. They should raise their hands to speak and wait to be called by the chairperson.

Vote

When everyone has had their say, the audience should vote on whether to agree to the development of tourism on Myssia.

Activity sheet 36

Role briefs

Foreign tour operators

You can see great benefits to your companies from tourism in Myssia. Lots of tourists want to holiday off the beaten track, and you could make a lot of money. You will need to stress:

- the benefits of the deal to the government and people
- the extra money for the people who will work for you
- the jobs that will come to the country, not only in the airport and tourist complex but also in shops and restaurants and in supplying the hotels with food, etc.
- that you might agree to contribute a large sum of money for a new hospital, which is needed.

Prepare a presentation for the meeting. Tell the people how you would develop the tourist resort and the benefits for them. You could draft plans and a drawing of the buildings.

Government of Myssia

Your country is desperate for income. There are many poor people and young people are leaving, but many do not have the education to get good jobs elsewhere. From the tour operators at the meeting you want guarantees:

- that there will be enough jobs to keep everyone employed
- that the jobs will go to local people
- that the tour operators will pay towards education and training so that people can get skilled jobs in the tourist trade
- that Myssia will not be spoiled by hoards of tourists coming every year.

Religious leaders

The people of Myssia are deeply religious and have a strict moral code of behaviour. Young men and women do not spend time together alone before they are married and they cover their bodies at all times. You have heard about tourists and are worried that:

- your young people will learn bad habits
- tourists will uncover their bodies and dress in ways that are offensive to your religion
- tourists will not treat the temples and statues with respect
- the people of Myssia will become more interested in material goods and things like cars and pop music, and will turn away from the simple life that is the basis of your beliefs.

Unemployed people

You have not been able to get work in fishing and your family is too poor to support you on its small plot of land. You would like to leave the country to get a job on the mainland. However, you have a very basic education and you speak only Myssese. If tourism came to Myssia your concerns are:

- What jobs will be available?
- Will you get one? You have heard that in other places outsiders have been brought in to do the best jobs because they have the skills and experience.
- Will the tour operators provide training to teach you these skills?
- Will the government help you to set up businesses, for example selling craft goods to tourists?

This is Citizenship 1 Teacher's Resource Book © Hodder Education, 2008

Activity sheet 36 (continued)

Local farmers, fishermen and pearl divers

At the moment, you can just about make ends meet from farming, fishing and diving for pearls. But fish stocks have suffered recently from a strange disease and the world price of pearls has fallen. If you are a fisherman or pearl diver, you are worried that if tourism comes to Myssia:

- the fish might be badly affected by watersports and scuba divers
- your old houses along the quayside will be knocked down to build shops and restaurants.

If you are a farmer, you are worried that:

- your land might be taken from you
- the hotels might use all the scarce water.

On the other hand, you will probably all be able to:

- sell your produce – pearls, fish, meat and vegetables – to hotels and restaurants and to tourists
- hire out your boats for fishing and diving, trips, etc.

Elders

You have lived all your life in Myssia and love it. You love the quiet, the beauty and the friendliness of the people. You do not want your country to change, although you know that things will be different for your grandchildren. You have mixed feelings:

- you do not want your country's beauty to be spoiled
- you do not want to see your religious traditions lost.

But you are very poor, so:

- you would like to feel that there will be money in the family to look after you in your old age
- you would like your young relations to be able to earn a living without having to leave the country.

Parents of young children and teenagers

You are worried about the future and how your children will be able to survive. Most of you have farmers and fishermen in your family. There is not enough work for everyone. You have mixed feelings about tourism:

- tourism might provide jobs
- tourist taxes might help the government build more schools
- you are worried about the likely increase in crime which you have been told often accompanies tourism
- you have relatives abroad who have told you about the ways tourists sometimes behave.

International environmentalists

Myssia is home to many rare and endangered species. You are certain that tourism will threaten the animal and plant life on land and in the ocean. The airport site would certainly destroy habitats. You also believe that holiday developments have spoiled the natural beauty of many parts of the world. You think the government should oppose the tour companies or limit the damage by putting strict restrictions on the tourist development. At the meeting you want to stress:

- the threat to wildlife
- the threat to the culture of the country, its religion and the traditional ways of doing things
- the way that when tourism arrives, some people earn lots of money while others do not, and this tends to cause arguments and splits in society.

Activity sheet 37

Prompt sheet

Foreign tour operators

- You will promise the people of Myssia all sorts of things, but you know that once the project gets going you can go back on your promises.
- You can lie about the impact of tourism. For instance, tell them that lots of jobs will go to the people of Myssia, whereas in reality you intend to bring in more experienced staff to run the hotels and other leisure facilities.
- Say you will build a hospital and a school. The hospital will be good for the tourists and the school will help educate the people of Myssia to fill jobs in the future.
- Promise that you will look carefully at what the fishermen and farmers ask for, but in reality you will bring in watersports and take over a lot of their land.
- Your aim is to make as much money as you can out of the project, but you are prepared to make compromises. For example, you are prepared to take local food and fish and protect the wildlife as you can use this in your marketing of holidays. But you cannot let the people dictate to you how you build or run your holiday complexes.

Government of Myssia

- You know that some parts of the country are going to suffer but believe that the country as a whole will benefit from the development of tourism.
- Some of you might get a lot of money because you are going to be in powerful positions. You want to know what you can get out of the tour operators. Talk to them privately, not in the meeting.
- Some members of the government are very worried about environmental damage, but others don't care much, as long as Myssia gets money and jobs. They believe that poverty is much worse than environmental problems.
- You can lie to the other groups in the meeting. Sometimes you think it's best that the people don't know the whole story. You want to make sure the project goes ahead.

Religious leaders

- Demand from the government that there are rules about how religious buildings should be treated by tourists.
- Demand that tourists should wear decent clothes when walking about the towns and villages.
- You do not want any loud music or nightclubs that you have heard about in neighbouring countries.

This is Citizenship 1 Teacher's Resource Book © Hodder Education, 2008

Activity sheet 37 (continued)

Unemployed people

- You want jobs and are glad to be able to stay on Myssia instead of being forced to leave.
- You want good jobs, not just ones like cleaning and working in the kitchens.
- You want the tour operators to guarantee that they will employ large numbers of local people and that they will pay them good wages.
- You want to try to push the tour operators to provide training so you have a chance to get better jobs.

Local farmers, fishermen and pearl divers

- You want guarantees from the tour operators and the government that you will be able to keep your boats and your land.
- You don't want watersports that might drive away the fish and ruin your pearl beds. Try to get the tour operators to promise they will not create large watersports areas.
- See if you can get some promises about the hotels and restaurants taking your fish and the food you grow.

Elders

- Ask the government how they are going to make sure that the countryside is not ruined by new developments.
- You want the ancient crafts to be protected so that young people learn the old skills.
- You want the tour operators and the government to set limits on the amount of new development until its effect becomes clear.

Parents of young children and teenagers

- You want to know what educational institutions are going to be built.
- You want to know if your children will get jobs in the future and what training will be available.
- You want to know how the government is going to deal with crime, which is not a problem in Myssia at the moment.

International environmentalists

- Other examples of tourist development have shown that people have been brought in from outside to run the hotels and other tourist operations. You want guarantees that local people will benefit.
- You want to try to make the government and the tour operators sign agreements to protect the environment and ensure that the wildlife won't be affected.
- You want to force the tour operators to agree to protect ancient buildings and submit their plans to the people for agreement.

© Hodder Education, 2008 *This is Citizenship 1 Teacher's Resource Book*

Resources

There is a wide range of resources available on all aspects of citizenship as well as a huge number of information sources. In fact, researching any issue can be a daunting and time-consuming experience. We have selected the websites below because they are useful for the topics covered in *This is Citizenship 1* and also provide gateways to other resources. We have only included websites because most information and resources are now accessible through them.

Websites

- ActionAid – information about anti-poverty campaigns, good on global education: www.actionaid.org
- Anti-Slavery International – information, case studies of modern slavery and people trafficking, also information about mounting campaigns: www.antislavery.org
- BBC CitizenX – basic information about citizenship topics, animations and activities, good for classroom sessions: www.bbc.co.uk/schools/citizenx
- BBC Newsround – latest news for children, good for discussing topical issues: http://news.bbc.co.uk/cbbcnews/default.stm
- British Red Cross – good ideas for campaigning and fundraising events: www.redcross.org.uk
- Britkid – anti-racism site aimed at young people: www.britkid.org/
- CAFOD – information on global issues, youth section, good on campaigning: www.cafod.org.uk
- Christian Aid – information about global issues at www.christian-aid.org.uk; also 'global gang' for younger pupils contains information about children around the world: www.globalgang.org.uk
- CitizED – all sorts of issues about teaching citizenship and reviews of resources: http://www.citized.info/index.php
- Citizenship Foundation – great source of information and resources as well as running a range of projects: www.citizenshipfoundation.org.uk/
- Comic Relief – resources (activities and video clips) and ideas for organising fundraising events: www.comicrelief.com
- Curriculum Online: search engine for citizenship resources: www.curriculumonline.gov.uk/Subjects/Ci/Subject.htm
- Education Guardian – links to wide range of sites: http://education.guardian.co.uk/netclass/schools/citizenship/0,5607,97539,00.htm
- Global Express – for young people to help them understand how news stories from the developing world happen, also information on campaigns like Make Poverty History: www.dep.org.uk/ge/gehome.php
- Institute for Citizenship – information on active citizenship, support for schools and resources for teaching citizenship topics: www.citizen.org.uk
- Manchester Development Education Project (DEP) – looks at issues regarding developing world such as social justice, diversity, sustainable development and poverty, resources and projects, also a Citizenship Education Project: www.dep.org.uk/
- Oxfam – great site for a wide range of educational resources on global issues, especially 'Milking It' for interactive white boards: www.oxfam.org.uk/education/
- Reading International Solidarity Centre (RISC) – information and resources on fair trade, sustainable development and social justice: www.risc.org.uk
- Recycle Zone – information and activities on waste, recycling and sustainable development: www.recyclezone.org.uk/
- Save the Children – information on children's rights and issues as well as teaching resources: www.savethechildren.org.uk
- SchoolNet Global – helps children learn about other cultures around the world: www.schoolnetglobal.com/

Resources

- School Councils Website – www.schoolcouncils.org
- Teachernet – provides a gateway to a range of resources and lesson plans on different subjects, including citizenship: www.teachernet.gov.uk/
- UNICEF – information about and case studies of children's rights around the world and resources: www.unicef.org/voy/index.php